59
S

BEHIND THE LINES

A SOURCEBOOK ON THE CIVIL WAR

BEHIND
THE LINES

A SOURCEBOOK ON THE CIVIL WAR

Edited by Carter Smith

AMERICAN ALBUMS FROM THE COLLECTIONS OF
THE LIBRARY OF CONGRESS

THE MILLBROOK PRESS, *Brookfield, Connecticut*

Cover: The camp of the 3rd Kentucky Infantry near Corinth, Mississippi. Lithograph by M. & N. Hanhart, 1871, after a painting by Conrad Wise Chapman, 1862.

Title Page: "Our Heaven Born Banner." Lithograph by Sarony, Major, & Knapp, after a painting by William Bauly, 1861.

Contents Page: Advertisement, "Soldier's True Friend, Holloway's Ointment and Pills."

Back Cover: "Death of Col. Ellsworth." Lithograph by Currier & Ives, 1861.

Library of Congress Cataloging-in-Publication Data

Behind the lines : a sourcebook on the Civil War / edited by Carter Smith.
     p. cm. — (American albums from the collections of the Library of Congress)
    Includes bibliographical references and index.
    ISBN 1-56294-265-4 (lib. bdg.)
    1. United States—History—Civil War, 1861–1865—Social Aspects—Juvenile literature. 2. United States—History—Civil War, 1861–1865—Social aspects—Pictorial works—Juvenile literature. 3. United States—History—Civil War, 1861–1865—Social aspects—Sources—Juvenile literature. I. Smith, C. Carter. II. Series.
E468.9.B34 1993
973.7—dc20   92-16662
                                                    CIP
                                                          AC

 Created in association with Media Projects Incorporated

C. Carter Smith, *Executive Editor*
Lelia Wardwell, *Managing Editor*
Elizabeth Prince, *Principal Writer*
Charles A. Wills, *Consulting Editor*
Kimberly Horstman, *Picture and Production Editor*
Lydia Link, *Designer*
Athena Angelos, *Photo Researcher*

The consultation of Bernard F. Reilly, Jr., Head Curator of the Prints and Photographs Division of the Library of Congress, is gratefully acknowledged.

Manufactured in the United States of America.

10 9 8 7 6 5 4 3 2 1

Contents

Millions of families were torn apart by the Civil War. In this Currier & Ives print, a Northern family prepares for the father's departure for the front. A framed painting of charging cavalry hangs on the wall, suggesting that military service was important in the nineteenth-century United States. In fact, most Americans felt that large armies posed a threat to personal liberties.

Introduction

BEHIND THE LINES is one of the volumes in a series published by The Millbrook Press titled AMERICAN ALBUMS FROM THE COLLECTIONS OF THE LIBRARY OF CONGRESS, and one of six books in the series subtitled SOURCEBOOKS ON THE CIVIL WAR.

The editors' basic goal for the series is to make available to the student many of the original visual documents preserved in the Library of Congress as records of the American past. The volumes in THE CIVIL WAR series reproduce prints, broadsides, maps, paintings, and other works from the Library's special collections divisions, and a few from its general book collections. Most prominently featured in this series are the holdings of the Prints and Photographs Division.

BEHIND THE LINES introduces many of the prints produced for, and portraying life on, the home front during the Civil War. These prints served as propaganda for both the Northern and Southern causes. Sentimental scenes of noble husbands taking leave of their wives and children provided encouraging, if unrealistic, models for the families of soldiers off fighting in the Union Army. Adalbert Volck's Confederate war etchings (pages 37 and 46) fulfilled much the same function for the Confederacy.

The heroic deeds of the men in the field, though real, were presented by artists in ways that did not accurately portray the confusion and mayhem that often engulfed the actual events. The death of Elmer Ellsworth, for instance, the first Union officer killed in the war, was commemorated by scores of Northern artists, who cast Ellsworth as a martyr of religious dimensions and his attacker as a treacherous scoundrel. As the labels and tradecards shown here attest, the art of advertising was similarly infused with the patriotic spirit.

Even in the North, artists were both loyal to and critical of the Union cause. The rise of the Copperheads, or Peace Democrats, in 1863 provoked scornful commentary from pro-Republican cartoonists. And the Irish anti-draft rioters of 1863 were portrayed as ape-like brutes. Lincoln's Emancipation Proclamation was celebrated with a number of pictures by those who saw the war as a crusade against slavery. It was in these grand allegories (such as on page 41) that Lincoln's image began to change from the rustic railsplitter of the 1860 campaign to a national savior and champion of the African-American race.

In the extensive pictorial documentation of the Civil War, scenes of camp life proliferated. Photographs by Brady and Gardner and informal studies by Alfred Waud and Edwin Forbes convey a great deal about the texture of life in the ranks of the Union Army. Due to the duration of the Civil War and the large percentage of the population involved, it was the first conflict in American history in which everyday life off the battlefield was recorded.

The works reproduced here represent a small but telling portion of the rich pictorial record of the Civil War preserved by the Library of Congress in its role as the nation's library.

BERNARD F. REILLY, JR.

Through diplomacy, purchase, and the spoils of war, the United States had expanded into a continent-wide network of states and territories by the middle of the nineteenth century.

The contest over slavery and its extension into the Western territories finally tore the nation apart in 1861. The border states of Maryland, Kentucky, and Missouri—slave states that remained loyal to the Union—made an uneasy buffer between the warring North and South.

The thread that connected the Far West to the Confederate states was the Mississippi River, running from northern Minnesota down through New Orleans and finally into the Gulf of Mexico. Control of the Mississippi River was a key goal of Union strategy throughout the war. When the Union completed its conquest of the Mississippi in the summer of 1863, the Confederacy was effectively cut in half.

While the North and South waged war for the control of the Mississippi, homesteaders continued to move into the West, populating new states and territories such as Nevada, New Mexico, and Colorado. In 1862, Congress took time out from the war to pass two far-reaching laws that encouraged Western settlement. The first, the Homestead Act, gave away millions of acres of the frontier to those willing to settle on it. The second authorized construction of a transcontinental railroad to the West Coast. When the railroad was completed—in 1869, four years after the war's end—it helped tie the reunited nation together.

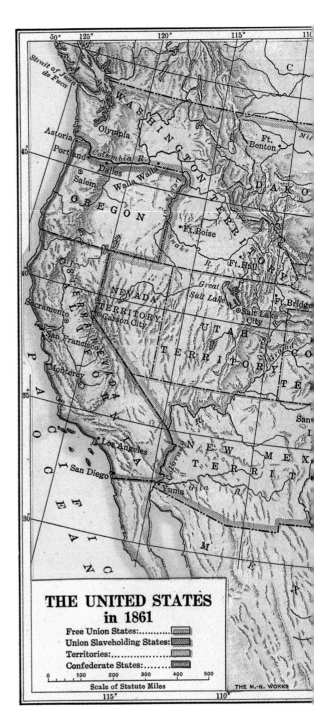

THE UNITED STATES
in 1861

Free Union States:...........
Union Slaveholding States:
Territories:.................
Confederate States:........

Scale of Statute Miles

THE M.-N. WORKS

BEHIND THE LINES

April 15, 1861 President Lincoln calls for 75,000 state militia troops to crush the rebellion. The Confederacy has already assembled a volunteer army of 60,000 soldiers.
•In New York City, 250,000 people turn out for a Union rally. The press calls this display of patriotism "miraculous," as New York is known for its pro-Southern sympathies.
•The secessionist governor of Missouri calls Lincoln's request for troops "illegal, unconstitutional, revolutionary, inhuman."

Queen Victoria

April 23 In Richmond, the women of Grace Baptist Church meet after Sunday services to form a sewing society. Sewing circles spring up throughout the South, hand-producing everything from blankets to sandbags for the war effort.

April 29 Three thousand women meet in New York City to organize the Women's Central Association for Relief (W.C.A.R.).

May 6 The Confederate government declares war on the United States. (To deny the authority of the Southern government, President Lincoln uses the term "insurrection" rather than "war.")

May 15 Queen Victoria declares that Britain will remain neutral, despite the importance of Southern cotton to Britain's textile industry.

May 23 Virginia— the largest and most prosperous Southern state—

MILITARY EVENTS

April 11, 1861 South Carolina authorities demand Fort Sumter's surrender. Union commander Major Robert Anderson refuses. Bombardment begins early on April 12; Anderson, out of food and water, finally surrenders the badly battered fort on April 13.

April 17 Jefferson Davis authorizes armed Southern vessels to seize Northern merchant ships. By July, two dozen Yankee ships have been captured by Confederate raiders.

April 18 Union general in chief Winfield Scott offers Colonel Robert E. Lee command of the Union Army; Lee does not accept.

April 19 A Massachusetts regiment traveling through Baltimore is attacked by a secessionist mob. Three soldiers and eleven civilians are killed.
•President Lincoln declares a naval blockade of all Confederate ports.

May 3 General Winfield Scott outlines what is quickly called the "Anaconda Plan" to defeat the South; the strategy calls for the Union to first isolate and then strangle the Confederacy by a naval blockade combined with control of the Mississippi River.

May 10–11 Riots between pro-Union and secessionist mobs sweep St. Louis, Missouri. A determined effort by Captain Nathaniel Lyon defeats pro-South forces.

May 24 Union troops occupy Alexandria, Virginia; Colonel Elmer Ellsworth is killed while tearing down a Confederate flag; he is the first person killed in the war.

July 14 A Union force under

officially secedes from the Union.

June 10 Dorothea Dix, well known for her efforts to improve conditions in hospitals for the mentally ill, is appointed Superintendent of Nurses for the Union Army.

June 13 Lincoln establishes the U.S. Sanitary Commission. Staffed largely by female volunteers, the Sanitary Commission is devoted to improving medical

Chimborazo Hospital

care and living conditions in Union Army camps.

June 19 Citizens of the western counties of Virginia vote to stay in the Union, even if it involves forming a new state.

November Chimborazo Hospital is established in Richmond. The facility becomes the world's largest military hospital—with 250 pavilion buildings, each housing about forty to fifty patients.

November 6 Jefferson Davis is formally elected president of the Confederacy. His vice president is Alexander Stephens.

December 3 In his annual message to Congress, President Lincoln recommends that "steps be taken" to colonize the slaves who have entered into Union lines, and to aid any freed slaves who might wish to leave the United States.

The death of Col. Edward Baker

General Irwin McDowell advances on the Confederate Army at Manassas Junction, Virginia.

July 21 The First Battle of Bull Run is fought. After initial success, McDowell's army is defeated, and the survivors begin a chaotic march back to Washington.

August 10 Confederates defeat forces led by Nathaniel Lyon in the Battle of Wilson's Creek, Missouri. Lyon dies in the fighting.

August 20 General George McClellan assumes command of the Army of the Potomac, the largest Union fighting force.

August 27 Union forces capture Cape Hatteras on the North Carolina coast. The landing greatly strengthens the Union's blockade of Southern ports.

October 21 Union troops are defeated at Ball's Bluff on the Potomac River. Among those killed is Colonel Edward Baker, senator from Oregon and friend of President Lincoln.

November 1 General Winfield Scott resigns as general in chief of Union forces; General George McClellan assumes overall command of the Union war effort.

November 7 A combined army-navy operation leads to the capture of Port Royal, North Carolina, by Union forces.

A TIMELINE OF MAJOR EVENTS
January 1862–December 1862

BEHIND THE LINES

January 31, 1862 Congress authorizes President Lincoln to seize railroad and telegraph lines for the war effort.

March 6 Lincoln asks Congress to consider compensating slaveowners who voluntarily free their slaves. The reaction from border state politicians is lukewarm.

March 13 Congress passes an article of war forbidding army officers to return fugitive slaves to their masters.

April 16 The Confederate government authorizes a draft to fill the ranks of its armies

May 9 Union general David Hunter issues a sweeping declaration of martial law, abolishing slavery in South Carolina, Georgia, and Florida. President Lincoln (who learns of this ac-tion through the newspapers) cancels Hunter's declaration.

May 16 General Benjamin Butler, commander of the Union forces occupying New Orleans, issues an order stating that any woman showing disrespect for his troops will be treated as "a woman of the town." He is nicknamed "Beast" by outraged Southerners.

May 24 Stonewall Jackson's troops seize 15,000 cases of chloroform in the Shenandoah Valley. Medical care for the Confederate wounded is greatly improved by the capture.

July 1 Congress passes the Internal Revenue Act of 1862. New tax laws go into effect in the North. In addition to an income tax, there are also taxes on such items as yachts and billiard tables, and "sin" taxes on tobacco, alcohol, and playing cards.

MILITARY EVENTS

January 19, 1862 The Union drives Confederate forces from the eastern part of Kentucky in the Battle of Mill Springs.

February 6–16 General Grant's troops, assisted by gunboats commanded by Commodore Andrew Foote, capture forts Henry and Donelson on the Tennessee River.

February 8 A naval battle off Roanoke Island, North Carolina, ends in a Union victory; Union troops under General Ambrose Burnside succeed in capturing the island.

March 7-8 The Battle of Pea Ridge, the most important clash west of the Mississippi River, is fought in Arkansas.

March 9 The Union ironclad *Monitor* engages the Confederate ironclad

Fort Donelson after its surrender

Merrimack in combat off Hampton Roads. Their fight, the first battle ever fought by ironclad warships, ends when the *Merrimack* moves out of range of the *Monitor*'s gun.

April 6–7 The Battle of Shiloh (called the Battle of Pittsburg Landing in the South) is fought in southern Tennessee.

April 25 A Union naval expedition,

July 4 In a speech at Himrod's Corner, New York, black leader Frederick Douglass accuses Lincoln of

Frederick Douglass

halting "the anti-slavery policy of some of his most earnest and reliable generals."

August In a summer marked by violence between whites and blacks, Irish workers set fire to a Brooklyn tobacco factory. Most of the workers inside are black.

August 4 An Indiana delegation offers the U.S. government two black regiments. Lincoln rejects the offer, fearing that white

enlistments will decline in the border states.

September The Confederate Congress creates a law providing for civilian nurses in army hospitals. The act gives preference to women, previously thought too delicate to care for the wounded in time of war.

September 22 Following the Union victory at Antietam, President Lincoln issues the preliminary Emancipation

Proclamation. It states that as of January 1, 1863, all slaves in Confederate territory will be "forever free."

December 31 Congress agrees to admit the pro-Union counties of Virginia as a new state, named West Virginia.

led by Commodore David Farragut, captures New Orleans. The loss of the South's largest city is a major blow for the Confederacy.

June 8-9 After twin victories at Cross Keys and Port Republic, Virginia, Stonewall Jackson leaves the Shenandoah Valley to help General Lee defend Richmond from McClellan's advancing army.

June 25 The Battle of the Seven Days,

the major phase of the Peninsular Campaign, begins.

July 1 The Battle of the Seven Days ends when Union forces reach Malvern Hill and beat back a Confederate assault.

August 29–30 The Second Battle of Bull Run is fought at Manassas, Virginia. The Army of the Potomac, now led by General John Pope, is defeated by Lee and Jackson.

September 17 The Battle of Antietam is fought near Sharpsburg, Maryland. The battle becomes known as the single bloodiest day of the war.

October 4–6 Union forces under General William Rosecrans defeat a Confederate force near Corinth, Mississippi; the Confederates withdraw from Kentucky.

November 5 General Ambrose Burnside replaces McClellan as commander of

the Army of the Potomac.

December 13 The Battle of Fredericksburg ends in a costly defeat for the Union.

December 31 The Battle of Murfreesboro begins in Tennessee as Confederate forces under General Braxton Bragg attack positions held by Union troops.

BEHIND THE LINES

January 1863 General Nathaniel P. Banks, now Union commander in New Orleans, sets up rules to return contraband slaves to plantations as paid workers.

January 1 The Emancipation Proclamation goes into effect. The proclamation applies only to Confederate states, of which Tennessee and parts of Louisiana and Virginia are exempted.

January 27 Philadelphia newspaper editor A. D. Boileau is arrested for publishing anti-Union articles. Boileau is one of many Northern journalists and politicians arrested for spreading "disloyal sentiments."

February 25 To boost the Northern economy and to finance the war, Lincoln signs the Legal Tender Act into law. The Act sets up a national currency based on the purchase of government bonds.

March 3 Congress votes to suspend habeas corpus throughout the Union. Authorities can now arrest and hold criminal suspects without charge or trial. •Congress authorizes conscription. Those who can afford it avoid the draft by hiring a substitute or paying a fee.

April 1 Three thousand people riot in Richmond because of the high price and scarcity of food. The "bread riot" ends when Jefferson Davis appeals for calm.

April 2 The California state legislature votes to repeal the law barring blacks from testifying against whites in court.

May 5 Clement Vallandigham becomes a hero to the North's "Copperheads" (Northern opponents of the war) when he is charged with trea-

MILITARY EVENTS

January 3, 1863 The four-day battle at Murfreesboro in Tennessee finally ends with Bragg's Confederates withdrawing from the area, although Union forces suffer heavy losses.

January 26 Secretary of War Edwin Stanton authorizes the recruiting of black troops for the Union armies. Two Union regiments have already formed in Massachusetts.

The Alabama *and the* Kearsarge

January 29 General Joseph Hooker takes over command of the Army of the Potomac.

April 15 The Confederate commerce raider *Alabama* sinks two Northern whaling ships in the South Atlantic. The *Alabama* is searching the seas for Union ships in order to capture and destroy valuable cargo.

May 1 The Confederate Congress announces that captured black Union soldiers will be executed or, if slaves, returned to their owners.

May 4 The four-day Battle of Chancellorsville ends. The Southern victory is marred when Stonewall Jackson is accidentally wounded by his own troops. He dies six days later from pneumonia.

June 9 General J.E.B. Stuart's Confederate troopers clash with Union horsemen at Brandy Station,

Clement Vallandigham

son for publicly protesting the war.

July 1 Missouri abolishes slavery within its borders.

July 13 Rioters in New York City,

mostly Irish immigrants, turn against the city's blacks, whom they hold responsible for the war.

July 30 Hearing that captured black soldiers are being sold into slavery, Lincoln declares that "for every one enslaved by the enemy, a Rebel soldier shall be placed at hard labor on the public works."

September The northwest branch of the Sanitary Commission spon-

sors a two week fundraising fair in Chicago, which nets over $100,000 for the Union cause.

September 25 In Mobile, Alabama, the Sisters of Charity, a religious order, run out of funds for their home for orphaned girls. Their appeal to buy essentials from the Yankees in occupied New Orleans is denied.

November 19 Lincoln delivers his famous "few words"

at the dedication of the National Cemetery at Gettysburg.

December At the Confederate States Laboratory in Richmond, women munitions workers successfully strike for a sixty-cent raise, bringing their wage to three dollars a day.

December 8 President Lincoln offers amnesty to Confederates who agree to free their slaves and take an oath of loyalty to the United States.

Virginia, in the largest cavalry battle of the war.

July 1 A Confederate patrol enters Gettysburg, Pennsylvania, in search of shoes. A skirmish with Union cavalry quickly grows into a full-scale battle.

July 3 The Battle of Gettysburg climaxes in a 15,000-man Confederate assault on the Union positions. The attack is quickly dubbed Pickett's Charge.

•Suffering the effects of a six-week-long siege, the Confederate garrison at Vicksburg prepares to surrender the city to Union forces.

July 4 Lee's army begins its retreat from Gettysburg.
•The twin victories at Gettysburg and Vicksburg turn the tide of the war in the Union's favor.

July 9 Confederate Port Hudson, Louisiana, surrenders to Union general Nathaniel Banks.

Union control of the Mississippi is now complete.

July 18 Union troops launch an assault on Fort Wagner outside Charleston, South Carolina. In the forefront of the attack is the famous 54th Massachusetts regiment, made up of black soldiers.

August 20 Confederate "irregulars" (guerrillas), led by Colonel William Quantrill, attack Lawrence, Kansas.

The town is practically destroyed, and almost 200 people are killed.

September 20 Bragg's Confederates attack and scatter much of Rosecrans's force as the Battle of Chickamauga continues.

November 24–25 The Battle of Chattanooga begins as Union troops under General Joseph Hooker win victories at Missionary Ridge and Lookout Mountain.

A TIMELINE OF MAJOR EVENTS
January 1864–April 1865

BEHIND THE LINES

1864 Physician Mary Walker is granted a commission in the Army Medical Corps. Her application had been denied since 1861.

February 15 The Confederate Congress authorizes $5 million for Canadian-based sabotage operations against the Union.

June 15 Congress grants equal pay to black soldiers.

June 24 Maryland officially abolishes slavery.

August The Democratic Party, calling for a "softer war," nominates General George McClellan for president.

August 23 Lincoln privately expresses doubts that he will be reelected. One factor is the dismal Union war effort; also, no incumbent president has been reelected since 1832.

November 8 Lincoln is reelected to the presidency. This unexpected victory is due partly to Sherman's successful campaign through Georgia and the Carolinas, which serves to cripple the Confederacy, hush Lincoln's opponents, and restore Northern confidence in Lincoln's administration.

Black troops

MILITARY EVENTS

March 8, 1864 President Lincoln promotes General U. S. Grant to the command of all Union forces.

March 15 The Red River Campaign opens in Louisiana; Union forces under General Nathaniel Banks move into western Louisiana and eastern Texas to keep the cotton-rich area from the Confederacy.

April 12 Confederate troops capture Fort Pillow, Kentucky. Over 230 of the Union defenders are killed by Confederates after the fort surrenders.

May 5-6 The Battle of the Wilderness, so named because of the dense woods in which the battle takes place, is fought in eastern Virginia.

May 8 The Confederate and Union armies clash again near Spotsylvania Court House in the opening skirmishes of what will become a four-day battle.

June 2-3 The Battle of Cold Harbor, Virginia, takes place.

June 19 The U.S.S. *Kearsarge* sinks the Confederate warship *Alabama* in the English Channel near Cherbourg, France.

July 17 Sherman's army arrives in front of Atlanta, Georgia, after a two-month-long march.

July 30 Union engineers explode a huge mine under the Confederate trenches outside the town of Petersburg, Virginia.

August 5 A Union fleet under Admiral David Farragut succeeds in capturing Mobile, Alabama, an important Confederate port.

September 19 General Philip Sheridan wins a major victory at Winchester in the

January 11, 1865 Missouri's state government orders that all slaves be freed.

January 16 Sherman sets aside large portions of the Southern coast as settlement areas for former slaves. By June, 40,000 freed men and women are settled on new farms.

January 31 Congress adopts the Thirteenth Amendment, which will abolish slavery throughout the United States when ratified by three fourths of the states.

February 1 Boston attorney John Rock, a black man, is sworn in by Chief Justice Salmon P. Chase for admission to practice before the Supreme Court.

March 3 Congress sets up the Freedmen's Bureau, which helps white Southern refugees rebuild their lives and helps millions of former slaves make the transition to freedom.

March 4 Lincoln is inaugurated for his second term as president.

March 13 Jefferson Davis authorizes the enlistment of black slaves as soldiers in the Confederate Army.

April 4 Escorted by black troops, President Lincoln tours Richmond shortly after its capture by Union forces. Although the city lies in ruins and is blackened by fire, Jefferson Davis urges Southerners to continue the fight against the Union.

April 14 Lincoln is shot by John Wilkes Booth while attending a play at Ford's Theatre in Washington, D.C. He dies early the next morning.

Shenandoah Valley.

November 16 Sherman's army leaves Atlanta on its "March to the Sea." He orders his troops to kill livestock, burn crops, and tear up railroads as they advance to the Atlantic Coast.

December 21 Sherman captures Atlanta and announces his victory as a "Christmas gift" for President Lincoln.

January 16, 1865 Fort Fisher, the South's last open port, falls to Union forces.

February 18 Confederate forces evacuate Charleston, South Carolina. The U.S. flag is finally raised again over Fort Sumter.

April 3 By day's end, both Richmond and Petersburg are securely in the Union's hands.

April 4–8 Union troops surround Lee near Appomattox Court House, Virginia.

April 9 Lee meets with Grant and accepts his terms for the surrender of the Army of Northern Virginia.

April 26 Confederate General Joseph E. Johnston surrenders his 30,000 troops—the last intact Southern army—to Sherman.

Shells exploding on the streets of Charleston, South Carolina

Part I
Politics and Civilian Life

Contrary to this idyllic view, nineteenth-century farming was backbreaking work that often went on seven days a week. But compared with the ordeal of combat, the family farm was an island of calm that conjured up images like this in the minds of weary, scared soldiers.

The Civil War changed the way Americans lived. In the North, the drive to manufacture vast quantities of war materials spurred industrialization. In the South, a rural economy based on slave labor was destroyed, plunging a once-prosperous region into decades of poverty. More than 800,000 Europeans—mainly from Germany, Ireland, and Britain—immigrated to the North, increasing its population despite its heavy casualties from the war. On both sides of the Mason-Dixon line, women began leaving their homes to work in munitions factories, in hospitals, and on farms.

Government became increasingly powerful. Draft laws requiring military service were instituted by both the Union and Confederate governments, along with taxes on goods and income. These measures undercut valued American beliefs about personal freedom from large, impersonal authority.

Union military strategy marked the beginning of modern warfare. The "total war" waged by the Union against the South was not confined to the battlefield. Now war was fought against an entire population, of which soldiers were only one part.

Most important, the war forced all Americans to renew their notions of liberty. In a few short years, abolitionism—the movement to end slavery—went from being a radical idea to becoming the defining principle of the war. The ratification of the Thirteenth Amendment in 1865, outlawing slavery throughout the nation, signaled the beginning of a struggle for equality that continues today.

CIVILIANS WATCH A BLOODY WAR BEGIN

When the bombardment of Fort Sumter in Charleston, South Carolina, began on April 12, 1861, thousands of civilians crowded the town square to celebrate the beginning of the war between the states. In New York City, well known for its pro-Southern sympathies, hundreds of thousands of loyal Unionists emerged. The patriotic revival sent citizens from all walks of life to recruiting offices. The 6th New York Regiment was made up almost entirely of streetwise toughs. One observer said that a recruit had to prove he'd done time in jail to be admitted. The 7th New York was exclusively upper-class: It set out for Washington with 1,000 velvet-covered camp stools.

In the South, planters' sons enlisted as privates and arrived at camp with slaves to wash and cook for them. Others, eager to prove a talent for leadership, recruited local regiments. In South Carolina, wealthy plantation owner Wade Hampton raised a regiment-sized "legion" of infantry, cavalry, and artillery at his own expense.

These men weren't thinking of the pain and loss of war. Nor were their wives and families, who busied themselves making flags and uniforms to accompany husbands, fathers, and brothers to the front. Each side believed that their rights had been trampled on. Both sides expected a clean, short fight. But soon enough, everyone would realize the war ahead would be both bloody and long.

Edmund Ruffin (1794–1865; above) was a Virginia farmer and an outspoken secessionist who leapt at the chance to aid the Rebel cause. An honorary member of South Carolina's Palmetto Guard, Ruffin is credited by some with firing the first shot at Fort Sumter. Unwilling to live in a defeated South, he killed himself on June 18, 1865.

With war fast approaching, the wives and children of the Union garrison at Fort Sumter leave for Fort Hamilton, New York, on February 3, 1861, as shown in this wood-engraving (below). The fort's defenders cheer as the steamship carrying them turns north, and Major Robert Anderson (1805–71), commander of the post, gives the departing families a twenty-one-gun salute.

THE SOUTHERN LEADERSHIP

Jefferson Davis was a veteran statesman who seemed an ideal choice for the job of Confederate president. He had served in Washington as a senator for Mississippi and as the secretary of war. When the Confederate Convention drafted him as president in February 1861, Davis—who hadn't expected to be chosen—appointed politicians from each seceded state to his cabinet to ensure regional support. His appointments, however, brought some of his harshest adversaries into the Confederate government. He even appointed arch-rival Robert Toombs of Georgia as secretary of state. And Confederate vice president Alexander Stephens came to despise Davis openly.

It was not easy to have faith in the Southern leadership. The Confederate Congress was notorious for infighting and inefficiency. It often met in secret, undermining the confidence of the public. Robert E. Lee, the South's leading general, once said that all Congress seemed to do was "chew tobacco and eat peanuts" while its ill-equipped armies starved.

Davis had signed on for an impossible job. He was trying to win a war and create a nation at the same time. The eleven states that eventually comprised this nation-in-the-making had little interest in federal government. Davis was routinely accused of violating states' rights, the very thing he was fighting to protect. His stern manner made it hard for him to inspire confidence in a wary public. As a political leader, Jefferson Davis never quite caught on.

As a West Point graduate, a former army officer, and a veteran of the Mexican War, Jefferson Davis (1808–89; above) considered himself as much a soldier as a statesman. He was personally responsible for the kinds of command decisions that Lincoln (who had little military experience) delegated to his generals.

In this wood-engraving, Jefferson Davis addresses the Confederate convention (opposite, top) in Montgomery, Alabama, on February 16, 1861, two days before his formal inauguration. The convention was a model of efficiency. In just six days, the delegates drafted a temporary constitution and elected a provisional president and vice president. (Davis's election was confirmed by popular vote in November 1861.)

The Confederate cabinet confers with General Robert E. Lee, leader of the Army of Northern Virginia, in this wood-engraving (right). The constant disputes within the Confederate government led to high turnover in the cabinet. In four years, the Confederacy had three secretaries of state and six secretaries of war.

THE NORTHERN LEADERSHIP

From the moment he took office in March 1861, Abraham Lincoln was guided by the central vision that the Union had to be preserved at all costs. But not everyone in the North agreed on what to do when war came. Lincoln had to appeal to a wide range of voters who had loud and often opposing views of what the North should fight for—or if it should fight at all. When the secession crisis first arose, some felt it would be better to let the South go its own way. Horace Greeley, editor of the influential *New York Tribune*, wrote, "If the Cotton States [are] satisfied . . . they can do better out of the Union, we insist on letting them go." Lincoln, however, believed that if secession prevailed, the Union was finished.

Like Jefferson Davis, Lincoln was troubled by conflicts within his own cabinet. Four of its members, including Secretary of State William Seward, had been Lincoln's rivals for the Republican presidential nomination in 1860. Others, like Secretary of War Simon Cameron, were appointed for purely political reasons. (The incompetent Cameron was replaced by Edwin Stanton in 1862.)

In addition to keeping the peace in his cabinet, the president had to tread a fine line in Congress: Some congressmen believed that the war should be fought only to preserve the Union, while others demanded that the abolition of slavery should be included in the North's goals.

During the war, the domeless Capitol Building (above) served as a symbol of an unfinished nation in the midst of great change. The dome was not completed until 1863. In the early months of the war, some Northern troops camped inside the Capitol itself.

This group portrait (right) shows Lincoln reading a draft of the Emancipation Proclamation to his cabinet in the summer of 1862. In addition to conflicts within his cabinet, Lincoln had to contend with Congress's Joint Committee on the Conduct of the War, which criticized many of the president's actions and interfered with the Union war effort.

CIVILIANS VERSUS SOLDIERS

An uneasy truce was maintained between civilians and occupying forces in Union-controlled parts of the South. The women of New Orleans had much contempt for Union troops. When, after Union forces took the city, an Ohio soldier offered to help a Confederate woman into her carriage, she slammed the door on his hand.

But much of the tension was between soldiers and civilians on the same side. The Southern government taxed poor farm families to feed the hungry Rebel armies. These civilians had no say as to the price they were given for food they couldn't spare. Insult was added to injury when they were paid in Confederate money, which was virtually worthless.

As the South's military efforts began to fail, tensions between Confederate soldiers and civilians increased. When Ulysses S. Grant's army drove Confederate forces into the defenses around Vicksburg in April 1863, angry women screamed, "Shame on you all!" as their tired defenders came onto the lines. Hungry Confederate troops scowled openly at the flag-waving women who did not offer them food.

In the North, enlistment efforts often met with violence. "Peace Democrats" opposed the state officials who tried to enforce draft quotas. Mobs murdered two enrollment officers in Indiana and wounded a commissioner in Wisconsin, while Union soldiers faced angry mobs in the massive Draft Riot in New York City in July 1863.

According to a legend that became a popular poem by John Greenleaf Whittier, ninety-six-year-old Barbara Frietchie boldly flew the Stars and Stripes as Confederate troops passed through Frederick, Maryland, in September 1862. A Confederate officer reportedly saluted her, tipping his hat and saying, "To you, madam, not your flag." This illustration (opposite, top) shows Frietchie in an inset portrait, along with a view of her grave (also displaying the American flag).

On April 19, 1861, the 6th Massachusetts Regiment entered Baltimore on its way to Washington, D.C. When a pro-secession mob attacked the soldiers with bricks, paving stones, and pistols, a few angry soldiers opened fire, as shown in this lithograph (right). Four soldiers and twelve civilians died in the riot that followed.

Twenty-four-year-old Elmer Ellsworth, a personal friend of Abraham Lincoln and his family, was the first officer to die in the Civil War. On May 24, 1861, Colonel Ellsworth spotted a Confederate flag flying from a hotel in Union-occupied Alexandria, Virginia. Ellsworth attempted to remove the flag, but the hotel keeper, James Jackson, shot and killed him (right). One of Ellsworth's men promptly retaliated, shooting Jackson. Widely reported on both sides, the incident made lasting heroes of both the colonel and the hotel keeper.

This photograph (below) shows the Marshall House Inn, site of the deadly confrontation between Jackson and Ellsworth. While Ellsworth's men occupied Alexandria, other Northern troops seized Robert E. Lee's handsome estate on nearby Arlington Heights. Today it is the site of Arlington National Cemetery.

SOUTHERN ECONOMIC PROBLEMS

With its agricultural economy, the South lacked the industrial capacity to produce war materials. Unable to export cotton because of the Northern blockade, and with less than $1 million dollars in specie (coin) in its treasury, the Confederacy raised money simply by printing it. This $1 billion in "printing press" money rapidly decreased in value. By 1864, a Confederate dollar had a gold value of only five cents. As the value of Confederate currency fell, prices soared, driving the price of scarce foodstuffs out of most people's reach. By 1862, salt was selling for $60 a bag. Farms suffered from a lack of salt, one of the only means of preserving meat. The situation grew so bleak that by the spring of 1862, "bread riots" began breaking out in Southern cities. The worst incident was the Richmond Bread Riot.

As the Confederacy's capital, Richmond's population had doubled since 1861, and the war had destroyed much of northern Virginia's farmland. Push came to shove on April 2, 1862, when more than a thousand women rioted in downtown Richmond, shouting "BREAD OR BLOOD!" One rioter told a well-dressed onlooker, "We celebrate the right to live. We are starving." Jefferson Davis appeared in person and ended the riot by threatening to have the militia open fire on the mob.

The Confederacy borrowed scarce cash from its citizens in an attempt to finance the war, especially through bonds like the one shown here (right), which is decorated with a portrait of Stonewall Jackson. The notes stated the date of repayment and the amount of interest that the purchaser was due. By 1862, however, most Southerners with cash to spare had only Confederate dollars—paper money of declining value, printed by the government. Over $150 million in bonds were issued by the Confederate government. None were ever repaid.

The Tredegar Iron Works (below) in Richmond was the largest industrial plant in the South. With the North's naval blockade cutting off imports, local manufacture of weapons was crucial to the Confederate war effort. It was mostly Southern women who "manned" these factories. Driven as much by economic hardship as by loyalty to the Southern cause, they earned $2.40 a day.

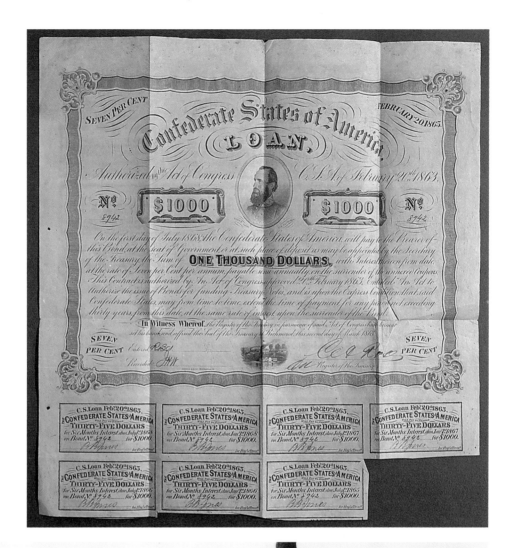

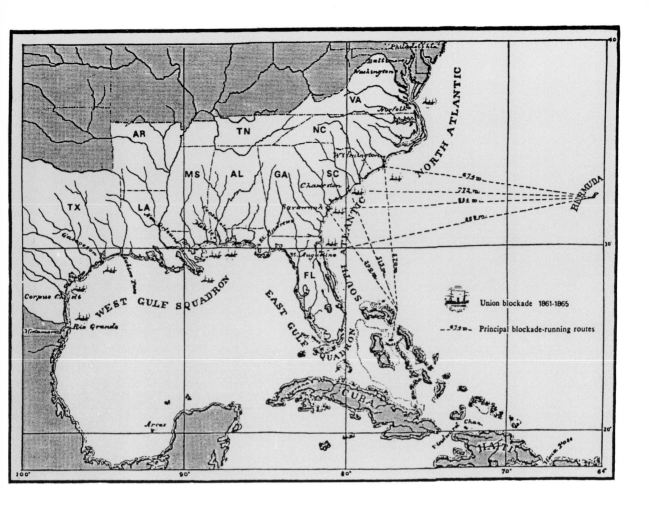

This map (left) shows the massive stretch of Lincoln's blockade of Southern ports. The blockade covered 3,500 miles and required hundreds of ships to enforce. With the Union Navy numbering only about ninety ships at the war's outbreak, many civilian vessels—from ferries to fishing boats—were hastily armed and pressed into service.

Blockade runners were fast steamships that slipped in and out of Southern ports, bringing precious cargoes of weapons, ammunition, and medicine to the Confederacy. Most blockade runners made it through in the early years of the war. By 1864, however, the Northern blockading squadrons were catching one runner out of every two. This drawing by A. R. Waud (opposite, bottom) depicts Confederate blockade runners in the harbor at Hamilton, Bermuda.

This 1862 Currier & Ives cartoon (below) ridicules the initial weakness of the Union's efforts at enforcing the blockade. (The cartoon calls the blockade the "Connecticut Plan," because Navy Secretary Gideon Welles was a native of Connecticut.) The Union Navy is pictured as a fleet of washtubs. Aboard the "steam-powered" tub, a sailor tends a large teakettle while his captain hails a blockade runner to demand its surrender.

THE BLOCKADE ON THE "CONNECTICUT PLAN".

NORTHERN INDUSTRY EXPANDS

When the Confederate states seceded, they took with them $300 million owed to Northern businessmen. The federal government, however, would eventually spend more than $2 million a day financing the war.

To raise money, Congress authorized sweeping tax measures, including the Internal Revenue Act of 1862, which authorized the first income tax in the nation's history. The government also issued "greenbacks"—paper money that Congress declared legal tender, although it was not backed by gold. One crucial difference between Union and Confederate economy was that gold and silver continued to flow into the Union's treasury from mines in California, Nevada, and Colorado. Eventually, the gold backed the paper.

The North's already vigorous industrial economy expanded to meet the needs of the Union Army and Navy, while its efficient farms were able to feed the nation and export wheat to Europe. In 1860, cotton exports had made up half the value of all American exports. Many predicted that the loss of the South's cotton would ruin the nation's foreign trade. By 1865, however, the Union's crop exports had more than made up for the loss.

Many Northerners prospered as factories scrambled to produce all the things needed to wage war—from locomotives and rifles to blankets and shoes. But wartime inflation kept most ordinary workers from reaping the benefits of this booming war economy.

In 1860, the Northern states produced ninety-seven percent of all arms and gunpowder in the United States. New York State alone had more factories than the entire South. The Confederate states had only about 9,000 miles of railroads, compared with 22,000 in the North. This industrial muscle would be decisive to the war's outcome. This lithograph (right) shows the flourishing Du Pont Gunpowder Plant on the Brandywine River in Delaware.

With access to both the Erie Canal and the Atlantic Ocean, New York City was the busiest harbor on the continent. During the Civil War, exports of wheat, flour, and corn from New York grew from 9 million bushels to 57 million bushels annually. This lithograph (below) shows New York Harbor, with the southern tip of Manhattan Island in the foreground.

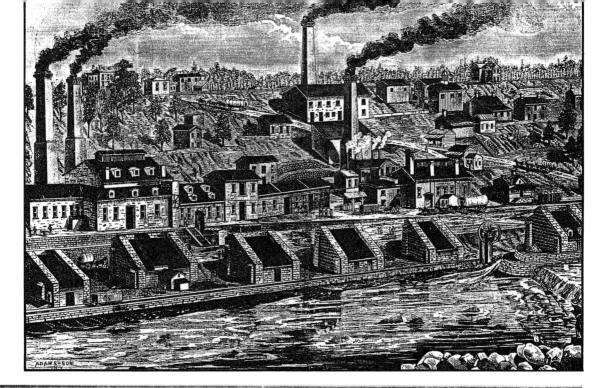

AFRICAN AMERICANS AND THE WAR

Black Americans played important roles in all aspects of the Civil War. Abolitionists such as Harriet Tubman, Frederick Douglass, and Pennsylvania physician John Rock were eloquent spokespersons for the Union cause. Because laws prohibited blacks from military service, they organized their own regiments while their leaders petitioned Congress to let them enlist. In New York City, an African-American group rented a public hall and began drilling until the threat of mob violence shut them down. The Union finally began enlisting black troops in 1862. By the war's end, 180,000 blacks had served in the Union Army and Navy— and more than 37,000 gave their lives for the Union cause.

From the South, about 500,000 fugitive slaves poured into Union lines over the course of the war, further weakening the Confederate economy. Nearly 200,000 of these former slaves, both men and women, assisted the Union armies as laborers. They worked in the fields on abandoned plantations, dug ditches, cooked for the troops, and cared for the wounded.

Throughout the war, and after, African Americans struggled to overcome white prejudice. White workers feared that the end of slavery would flood the market with black labor, driving wages down. In 1862, riots erupted in Ohio, Michigan, and Indiana, and many blacks were killed. During the New York draft riots in 1863, at least eleven blacks were murdered.

In 1861, Union general Benjamin Butler (1818–93) announced that he would treat slave refugees as "contraband [confiscated property] of war"; slaves entering Union lines in search of freedom were therefore called "contrabands." By the end of 1862, most Union army commanders had appointed a superintendent of freedmen (former slaves) affairs to oversee each contraband camp. The able bodied were employed as teamsters, hospital attendants, and company cooks. Ulysses S. Grant called this practice "saving soldiers to carry the musket." In this photograph (right), a group of contrabands pose outside their cabin.

Confederate artist Adalbert Volck drew this portrayal (opposite, bottom) of a devoted slave concealing her master from a Union patrol. While some slaves did have feelings of loyalty to their masters, most were joyful when Union troops approached—bringing freedom with them.

This photograph (below) shows a fugitive slave family crossing the Rappahannock River into Union-held territory in Virginia, their wagon sagging from the weight of family members and belongings.

TO FREE
THE SLAVES

Many Northerners, both white and black, argued that slavery was a source of strength to the Confederacy. Black activist Frederick Douglass urged the North to "turn this mighty element of strength into a weakness" by pursuing a policy of emancipation—freedom for the slaves.

By 1862, Union leaders were beginning to see Douglass's point. There was a growing belief that the fate of the nation could not be separated from the fate of slavery. In a speech on January 14, 1862, Republican senator George Julian noted that the Confederacy's four million slaves "cannot be neutral . . . they will be the allies of the Rebels, or of the Union." By summer, key pieces of antislavery legislation began arriving before Congress. On March 13, 1862, a new Article of War was passed forbidding army officers to return fugitive slaves to their masters. On April 10, Congress passed a resolution offering aid to any state that agreed to abolish slavery. Congress also voted in April to abolish slavery in Washington, D.C., prompting Frederick Douglass to exclaim, "I must be dreaming."

One of the most important early pieces of antislavery legislation was the Confiscation Act of July 1862. This bill ordered that slaves of anyone "engaged in rebellion against the United States" must be freed. To free slaves as a military measure against the South struck at the heart of the Confederacy, and paved the way for the Emancipation Proclamation.

Frederick Douglass (1818–95; above) worked tirelessly for emancipation after escaping from slavery at the age of twenty. Urging the enlistment of black troops, he wrote: "Once let the black man get upon his person the brass letters, U.S.; let him get an eagle on his button, and a musket on his shoulder, and there is no power on earth which can deny that he has earned the right to citizenship."

In this painting (right), a freedman reads news of the Emancipation Proclamation. Because slaves were generally denied education, few slaves could read or write at the beginning of the war. Many Northern cities organized freedmen's aid societies, which sent teachers and missionaries to Union-controlled areas of the South, especially the Sea Islands off the coast of Georgia and the Carolinas. By the war's end, more than 200,000 freedmen had received instruction in reading and writing—a critical step on the road to freedom.

THE EMANCIPATION PROCLAMATION

Before 1862, Abraham Lincoln had favored gradual emancipation, offering financial compensation for those who willingly freed their slaves. Although he was opposed to slavery on moral grounds, Lincoln's chief goal was the restoration of the Union.

By mid-1862, however, Lincoln was beginning to think of emancipation as a means to victory. Battlefield defeats had brought Northern morale to an all-time low. Something had to be done to revive the Union's war effort.

In July 1862, Lincoln proposed a dramatic measure. He had decided to declare all slaves in the Confederacy free if the seceded states didn't return to the Union by 1863. His cabinet supported the measure, but Secretary of State William Seward persuaded Lincoln to wait until the Union Army won a major victory before making the measure official.

In September, the Union Army halted a Confederate invasion of the North in the Battle of Antietam. On September 24, the Emancipation Proclamation was made public, and on January 1, 1863, it became the law of the land.

Because it applied only to states "in rebellion," the proclamation left slavery intact in loyal Union slave states such as Maryland. It had no effect in the Confederacy, which of course refused to obey the Union president's decree. But the Emancipation Proclamation turned the Civil War from a conflict over secession to one against slavery.

This print shows Lincoln drafting the Emancipation Proclamation. The text of the final document justified emancipation as "an act of justice, warranted by the Constitution, upon military necessity." The London Times ridiculed the fact that the document applied only to areas in rebellion, stating, "Where he has no power, Mr. Lincoln will set the negroes free; where he retains power he will consider them as slaves."

THE COPPERHEADS

The Copperheads were Northerners, mostly Democrats, who favored reunion with the South through negotiation, rather than armed conflict. Their opposition to the war was solidly based in their opposition to the emancipation of slaves. Some "War Democrats" also opposed emancipation, but felt that a union could be achieved only through military victory.

Also known as "Peace Democrats," the Copperheads used the issue of emancipation to stand up to the Republicans. They believed they were defying what they felt was Republican tyranny, and they raised troubling questions about individual freedom in times of war.

The most celebrated civil liberties case of the war concerned Clement Vallandigham. A candidate for governor in Ohio, Vallandigham aroused fears among the working class that emancipation would lead to lower wages and the loss of jobs. In April 1863, General Ambrose E. Burnside, commander of the Department of the Ohio, declared that any person who committed "implied treason" would be arrested. At a campaign rally on May 1, Vallandigham denounced the war as "wicked, cruel and unnecessary." He was arrested, convicted of treason by a military court, and sentenced to death. Although Lincoln altered his sentence to banishment to the Confederacy, Vallandigham had succeeded in raising important questions regarding civil liberties. Could a speech be treason? And could a military court try a civilian?

This wood-engraving (right) shows Union soldiers arresting Copperhead Clement Vallandigham (1820–71). The circumstances of his arrest seemed to support charges that his Constitutional rights had been violated: He was roused from sleep in his hotel room, marched to jail barefoot and in his underwear, and tried by a military court in a state where civilian courts still functioned.

On July 13, 1863, a huge riot against the draft erupted in New York City, as shown in this drawing (opposite, bottom). The rioters, mostly Irish immigrants, objected to fighting a war to free blacks, whom they feared would come North and take their jobs. Stores were looted, buildings were burned, and blacks were harassed and killed. The rioting continued for three days before Union troops arrived from Gettysburg to contain the mob. Over 1,000 people were killed or injured, most of them rioters.

Union "two-year men"—soldiers whose enlistments were over—leave for home by train in this sketch (below). Some Northern leaders blamed the low rates of reenlistment and the high rates of desertion on the Copperheads' antiwar speeches and writings. "Must I shoot a simple soldier boy who deserts," asked Lincoln, responding to criticism of his handling of the Vallandigham incident, "and not touch a hair of the wily agitator who induces him to desert?"

NORTHERN WOMEN AND THE WAR

In the North, women entered the workforce in such occupations as civil service, manufacturing, agriculture, and spying. They distinguished themselves most in nursing. On April 29, 1861, physician Elizabeth Blackwell organized a meeting of 3,000 women in New York City, which resulted in the Women's Central Association for Relief (W.C.A.R.). The United States Sanitary Commission was founded out of the W.C.A.R. Composed of 7,000 local chapters devoted to tending the wounded and reducing the spread of disease in army camps, the commission was the most important institution developed by women in the course of the war.

Washington recognized the contributions women were making. In June 1861, Dorothea Dix was appointed superintendent of nurses for the Union Army. Dix established a minimum age of thirty for her corps of nurses, and specified that women be "plain in appearance." While most worked in hospitals, some nurses took their skills to the front. Mary Ann ("Mother") Bickerdyke tended to the sick and injured at nineteen different battle sites.

Others wanted to strike the enemy where they would be sure to feel it. Franny Wilson of New Jersey fought in disguise with Union troops for eighteen months before she was wounded at Vicksburg and "found out." Over the course of the war, at least 400 women on both sides were discovered posing as soldiers.

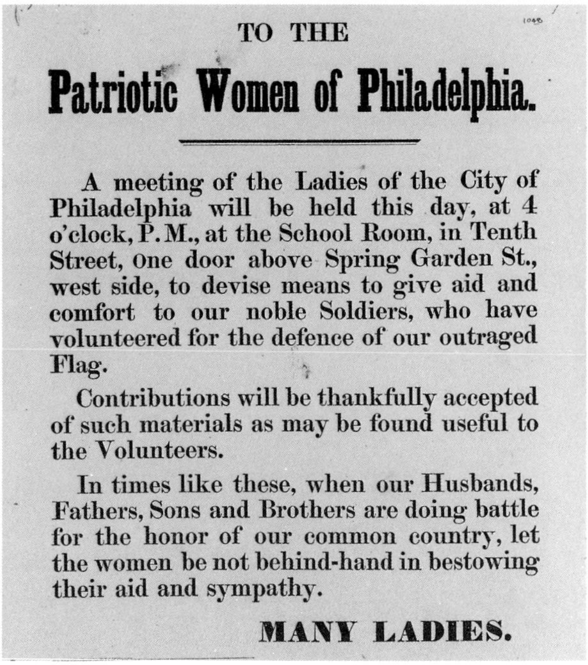

TO THE

Patriotic Women of Philadelphia.

A meeting of the Ladies of the City of Philadelphia will be held this day, at 4 o'clock, P. M., at the School Room, in Tenth Street, one door above Spring Garden St., west side, to devise means to give aid and comfort to our noble Soldiers, who have volunteered for the defence of our outraged Flag.

Contributions will be thankfully accepted of such materials as may be found useful to the Volunteers.

In times like these, when our Husbands, Fathers, Sons and Brothers are doing battle for the honor of our common country, let the women be not behind-hand in bestowing their aid and sympathy.

MANY LADIES.

Posters like the one shown here (above), appealing to the patriotism of women, dotted Northern cities. Historians estimate that Northern women's organizations raised about $50 million for the Union cause. One of the most influential groups was the National Women's Loyal League, founded by veteran women's rights activists Elizabeth Cady Stanton and Susan B. Anthony.

At the federal arsenal in Watertown, Massachusetts, the new labor force carefully fills cartridges with gunpowder, as shown in this wood-engraving (opposite, top) from Harper's Weekly. Even though women earned much less than men for the same or similar jobs, 100,000 Northern women found factory work during the Civil War. About 50,000 remained on the job after peace came.

Northern women were instrumental in organizing many of the local societies that provided nurses, blankets, clothing, medicine, and other necessities for Union soldiers. Most of these organizations were part of the U.S. Sanitary Commission, but many were from individual states and communities. This photograph (right) shows nurses of the Michigan Soldiers' Relief Society outside a field hospital.

SOUTHERN WOMEN AND THE WAR

Southern women bore nearly as much of the burden of war as the Rebel infantry. Their contributions to the cause were no less valiant or necessary. Sewing circles turned out everything from caps to sandbags, at times supplying entire regiments with uniforms, flags, and blankets. While most states furnished cloth for these projects, volunteer organizations had to find their own material after the first two years of the war.

As in the North, Southern women mobilized to care for the wounded. This action defied local custom, which considered nursing too indelicate for ladies. But when battles raged near Southern towns, whole communities opened up their homes to tend the wounded. Once military hospitals were established, women often had to help over the loud disapproval of male surgeons. Some doctors regarded them as evidence of a new "petticoat government." In Richmond, Sally Tompkins sidestepped this problem by starting her own infirmary. Jefferson Davis eventually awarded her a captain's commission. "Cap'n Sally" treated over 1,300 men during the war.

The South worked hard to develop industry that would meet wartime needs, and women were in the forefront. The Confederate Ordnance Department hired more than 500 women to fill cartridges. The work was dangerous, and explosions at two different factories killed over forty-five women.

Southern women spin, weave, and sew for the war effort in this Adalbert Volck drawing (above). Across the South, the Confederacy's quartermaster-general ran sweatshops to produce uniforms, paying only 30 cents a shirt and a quarter for underwear. Despite low wages and exhausting work, the government had no trouble finding applicants for 4,000 openings.

This print (opposite, top) shows, at left, wealthy women in fine dresses and bonnets waving their men down the steps and out into battle. At right, the now-hungry women are barefoot and in rags, smashing bakery windows to get bread. The images suggest that Southern women had helped start the rebellion and were responsible for the hard times they were now suffering.

Often the war brought tragic scenes to Southern homesteads and plantations. In June 1862, twenty-nine-year-old Captain William Latané was killed during J.E.B. Stuart's spectacular cavalry ride around the Army of the Potomac. His brother, also a Confederate trooper, arranged for the body to be buried at a nearby plantation. Two years later, William D. Washington painted this sentimental view of the simple burial service (right). The painting was exhibited in Richmond to raise funds for the Confederate war effort.

LIFE IN OCCUPIED NEW ORLEANS

Citizens of occupied areas were often forced to tolerate lawlessness and disrespect from invading troops. New Orleans, the South's largest city, was not known for its genteel manners. One local paper described the street gangs of New Orleans as "the most godless, brutal, and ruthless Ruffian[s] the world has ever heard of."

After the city fell to Union forces in April 1862, General Benjamin Butler became its military governor. Butler decreed martial law, hanged a gambler who tore down a Union flag, and confiscated the property of citizens who refused to swear allegiance to the Union. This earned Butler the nickname "Spoons," in honor of all the silver he was thought to have pocketed.

The women of New Orleans showed their displeasure at these actions. When a woman dumped the contents of her chamber pot directly on Flag Officer David Farragut's head, Butler issued his infamous General Order Number 28, which likened disrespectful women to prostitutes and stated that they would be legally treated as such. The action earned Butler another nickname, "the Beast," and made him the most hated man in the South.

But Butler's efficient rule of an unruly city had unexpected benefits. The strict enforcement of sanitation measures cleaned up the filthy streets and helped prevent the spread of yellow fever and other diseases. Butler also distributed Union rations to the city's poor. When he was replaced in December 1862, a newspaper called him "the best scavenger we ever had."

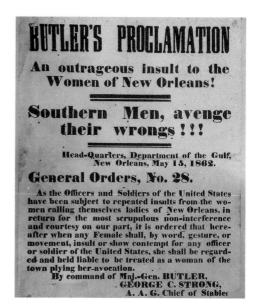

BUTLER'S PROCLAMATION

An outrageous insult to the Women of New Orleans!

Southern Men, avenge their wrongs!!!

Head-Quarters, Department of the Gulf,
New Orleans, May 15, 1862.

General Orders, No. 28.

As the Officers and Soldiers of the United States have been subject to repeated insults from the women calling themselves ladies of New Orleans, in return for the most scrupulous non-interference and courtesy on our part, it is ordered that hereafter when any Female shall, by word, gesture, or movement, insult or show contempt for any officer or soldier of the United States, she shall be regarded and held liable to be treated as a woman of the town plying her avocation.

By command of Maj.-Gen. BUTLER,
GEORGE C. STRONG,
A. A. G. Chief of Staff.

Butler's infamous proclamation (above) enraged not only the South but also members of the British Parliament. In an address to the House of Commons, Prime Minister Palmerston voiced outrage that such an act had been committed by "a member of the Anglo-Saxon race." Jefferson Davis declared him an "outlaw"—if captured, he was to be executed.

The citizens of New Orleans weren't easily conquered. When the victorious Union fleet anchored off the riverfront, they found that the city's stores of cotton had deliberately been set on fire. Angry crowds greeted the fleet, as shown in this wood-engraving (opposite, top). When the mayor refused to surrender the city, the fleet's commander, David Farragut, sent a party of Marines ashore to replace the Confederate flag with the Union stars and stripes.

This lithograph (right), titled "The Mississippi in Time of War," shows some of the destruction the Civil War brought to the Mississippi Valley. After securing New Orleans, Union forces moved upriver and captured Baton Rouge, Louisiana, and Natchez, Mississippi. Sarah Morgan, a young woman in Baton Rouge, was at first impressed by the Union occupiers. "These people," she wrote in her diary, "have disarmed me with their kindness." Her feelings changed when Union gunboats shelled the town in revenge for attacks by Confederate guerrillas.

SONGS OF WAR

Singing was a favorite pastime in nineteenth-century America. During the Civil War, millions of copies of sheet music were sold nationwide. The popularity of certain songs reflected the changing moods of both nations. In 1861, a favorite Union marching tune was "Yankee Doodle"; its upbeat chorus emphasized a "Can-Do" Yankee optimism. By late 1862, with freedom for the slaves emerging as a national goal, the favorite Yankee marching song was "John Brown's Body," glorifying the fallen abolitionist. When Lee marched through Union territory in Frederick, Maryland, the Army of Northern Virginia sang out "Maryland, My Maryland" to a lukewarm reception by pro-Union citizens.

In the early part of the war, with patriotic feeling running high on both sides, patriotic anthems such as "Dixie" and "The Bonnie Blue Flag" were popular in the South, as was "The Battle Cry of Freedom" in the North. By 1864, soldiers favored songs such as "Lorena" or "Tenting Tonight," which expressed the discomfort and homesickness of army life.

Other songs were written in protest. One Rebel soldier wrote a blistering attack on conscription, challenging a law that allowed those who could afford to escape service by paying substitutes to take their place. According to the chorus, "The men that was going to drink the blood, are not the men that wades the mud; Oh! no they'd rather stay at home; and send the innocents to distant lands to roam."

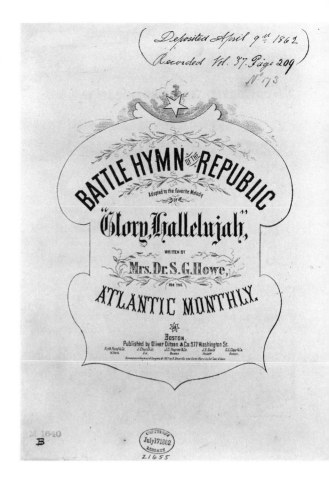

In "The Battle Hymn of the Republic" (above), one of the Civil War's most enduring songs, Julia Ward Howe gave voice to the growing belief of many Northerners that their own freedom was tied to freedom for the slaves. The morning after she witnessed a skirmish outside Washington in November 1861, Howe reported: "I awoke in the gray of the morning twilight, and as I lay waiting for the dawn, the long lines of the poem began to twine themselves." Set to the tune of the abolitionist song "John Brown's Body," it became a favorite of Union soldiers on the march.

In a flowing white gown, this angelic "spirit of the Union" is both strong and pure. Flanked on her right by a cannon and the American eagle, the woman on this sheet-music cover (left) was meant to symbolize the unstoppable resolve of the Union forces.

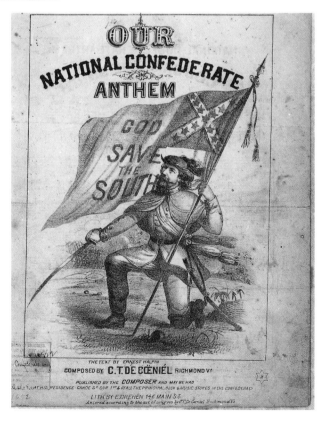

This sheet-music cover (right) depicts a gallant Confederate cavalryman, complete with sword and plumed cap, kneeling in service to the Confederacy. This Rebel knight bears little resemblance to the tattered fighting men of Antietam, Gettysburg, and other hard-fought battles.

WARTIME ADVERTISING

Although advertising in its modern form didn't emerge until late in the nineteenth century, the Civil War saw a huge rise in the use of advertisements to sell products, at least in the North. Before the war, advertisements were usually local. The wartime demand for news, however, led to an increase in the number of newspapers and magazines. By 1865, about 700 periodicals were in circulation. These periodicals turned to advertising as a way to boost revenue.

Advertising catered to the national obsession with war. Products were repackaged to reflect proper military zeal—the pocket watch was now an "Army Watch," which could be packaged "in a neat case." Ads were placed in national magazines to receive a "first class interesting newspaper" called the *Army and Home Journal.* Military heroes got in on the action, too, promoting such products as "Brooche's Patent Writing and Toilet Case," which Commander Cushing of the Union Navy endorsed.

The contrast between Northern and Southern advertising, however, was extreme. While Northern newspapers paraded items such as "American Steel Collars" and India rubber gloves, Southerners were struggling to buy salt, flour, and cloth. But advertising wasn't limited to selling the goods turned out by Northern industries. Financier Jay Cooke, acting on behalf of the U.S. Treasury, used patriotic ads to sell government bonds to raise money for the war. (Cooke also got a commission for every bond sold.)

Red Cross Bitters uses images inspired by war and heroism in this advertisement (above). A knight in armor, proudly displaying his sword and shield, stands triumphant beside the body of his conquered enemy.

No commodity was untouched by patriotic advertising. This ad (right) for Cuban cigars features a soldier cloaked in the Union flag, his saber outstretched as he charges boldly toward the enemy. Tobacco was one of the few consumer items in short supply in the North, as most of it was grown in the Confederate states. Rebel soldiers often traded tobacco to Union troops, receiving sugar or coffee in return.

During the Civil War era, self-appointed "doctors" concocted and sold scores of "patent medicines." Despite the exaggerated claims of their advertisements, these tonics, ointments, and pills rarely cured anything, and some were downright harmful. This advertisement (below) proclaims that Holloway's pills and ointments will bring "health for the soldier."

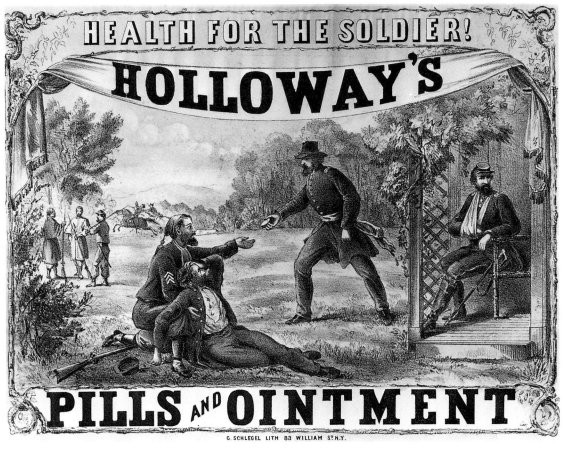

SPIES

Neither the Union nor the Confederacy had an organized intelligence operation when the war began. Each side recruited patriotic amateurs, some possessing more zeal than talent for spying. In the North, famous detective Allan Pinkerton volunteered to shield President-elect Lincoln from a suspected assassination attempt in Baltimore. After Fort Sumter, Pinkerton acted as intelligence chief for General George McClellan, commander of the Army of the Potomac. Although Pinkerton assembled an impressive collection of "operatives" (spies), his intelligence missions for McClellan were hampered by exaggeration. His men reported Southern troop strength far in excess of the actual numbers. Hearing that the enemy outnumbered him by two or three times, McClellan—already cautious—failed to move as quickly as he should have during the Peninsular Campaign of 1862.

In charge of Confederate intelligence was Major William Norris. Officially head of a signal bureau, Norris ran a spy network that extended to Montreal. The Confederacy was gifted with brave Southern women who added daring and ingenuity to Rebel spy operations. The best known was Belle Boyd, who became a celebrity by dramatizing her activities to the press.

Union troops found that one of the best sources of intelligence were slaves, who eagerly reported on Confederate troop movements. The great abolitionist Harriet Tubman also made several spying journeys behind Confederate lines during the war—for which she was paid only $200, despite the risk involved.

By socializing with the Union Officers who occupied her hometown of Martinsburg, Virginia, Belle Boyd (1843–1900; above) collected valuable intelligence from seemingly casual conversation. After her second arrest for espionage, she fled to England where, ironically, she married a Union officer.

Northern hotel lobbies provided an ideal setting for espionage. Off-duty officers gathered there for drinks and small talk with attractive women, some of whom were Confederate spies. This print (opposite, top) shows Willard's Hotel in Washington. Willard's was a favorite haunt of politicians and reporters, as well as officers, making it a rich source of intelligence.

Timothy Webster was one of the most effective Union spies. A former detective, Webster became famous for infiltrating Confederate operations in the South. Webster was betrayed by another Union agent eager to save his own neck. Webster wanted to be shot as a soldier rather than hanged as a spy, and fellow Northern spy and prisoner Hattie Lawton begged Confederate authorities to grant his last request, as shown in this print (right). Webster was hanged on April 29, 1862.

LINCOLN'S REELECTION

By the summer of 1864, Lincoln did not expect to be reelected. His campaign was dogged by Peace Democrats and by members of his own party who criticized the ailing Union war effort. In February, Republican senator Henry Pomeroy had publicly endorsed Treasury Secretary Salmon P. Chase for president. Lincoln's supporters counterattacked, trying to undermine Chase's credibility by claiming fraud in the treasury. Chase distanced himself from Pomeroy and offered to resign his cabinet post. Lincoln, however, refused his resignation. General John C. Frémont also opposed Lincoln, running as a Radical Republican. His campaign quickly folded.

Lincoln was nominated by a coalition of Republicans and War Democrats at what was nicknamed the "National Union Convention." His running mate was Andrew Johnson, a Southern War Democrat. The platform endorsed unconditional surrender for the Confederacy and an end to slavery.

Peace Democrats appealed to Northern war weariness in hopes of unseating the president. The Democratic Party nominated George McClellan for president on a peace platform stressing reunion through negotiation. McClellan's candidacy seemed invincible until William Tecumseh Sherman marched his army into Atlanta on September 2, 1864, announcing, "Atlanta is ours, and fairly won." With final victory much closer, a weary nation now wanted to see the war to the end, and Lincoln was elected to a second term in November.

Mathew Brady photographed a tired, thoughtful Lincoln just before his second inaugural address. It was the president's last portrait: he would die April 15, 1865, six days after Lee's surrender at Appomattox. Robert Todd Lincoln, the president's son, described this portrait (above) as "the most satisfactory likeness" of his father.

This photograph (opposite, top) shows Lincoln's second-term inauguration on March 4, 1865. In his inaugural address, Lincoln looked toward the end of the war and urged a spirit of healing for the divided nation. His speech ended: "With malice toward none, with charity for all; with firmness in the right, as God gives us to see the right; let us strive to finish the work we are in . . . to do all which may achieve and cherish a just and lasting peace, among ourselves, and among all nations."

George McClellan, the Democratic candidate in 1864, was a former commander of the Army of the Potomac. Although many of his former troops held him in high regard, the "soldier vote" went solidly to Lincoln. This drawing by A. R. Waud (right) shows Union troops casting their absentee ballots in camp. Other soldiers were given furloughs to vote in their home districts.

LIFE UNDER SIEGE

Some parts of the South, such as northern Virginia, saw almost constant fighting. In these areas, civilians were forced to adapt to the presence of hostile armies on their soil. Children were moved quickly into basements, where women slept fully clothed, often clutching butcher knives. Eventually many civilians began taking combat for granted. One Alabama woman watched the Union shelling of Spanish Fort in Mobile Bay from a third-story window before moving downstairs for a pleasant lunch with friends. Charleston, South Carolina, was under siege from the summer of 1863 until just before the war ended in 1865. Casualties and damage were fairly light, although Union shells crashed into the city from time to time.

But few cities could maintain a polite distance from enemy fire. During the Battle of Fredericksburg, in December 1862, one woman spent thirteen hours on a damp basement floor as shells ripped through the upper stories of her house. In 1863, during the siege of Vicksburg, most families endured the constant bombardment by the North by entrenching themselves in basements or in caves dug into the hillsides. But they could not hide from starvation. Families were finally reduced to eating mule meat and rats.

In this painting by Howard Pyle (above), a woman, her slave, and a Confederate soldier cringe in horror as a Union shell with a lighted fuse lands on a Vicksburg street. During the long siege of Vicksburg, a survivor wrote, "all lived in terror." Despite six weeks of bombardment, however, only a dozen civilians were killed before the besieged city surrendered.

Adalbert Volck sketched this view of Union troops looting a Southern home (opposite, top). A drunken officer taunts a mother and child with a Union flag, while a man, still in his bedclothes, is restrained by soldiers. While some Union officers took pains to ensure that civilians were unharmed and private property left alone, the sketch shows another side of the story.

When word spread that the Union troops were coming, many Southern families decided to take their chances and flee into the woods. This wood-engraving (right) shows an assembly of women with children and slaves camped outside Vicksburg. A Rebel cavalryman brings them news from the front.

TOTAL WAR

By the time General Sherman began his march from Atlanta to the sea in November 1864, the Confederacy was brutally aware of the meaning of total war. Georgian women, defending their homes single-handedly or with the help of children and reluctant slaves, prepared for the worst. First they hid valuables. Jewelry and silver went into mattresses, wells, flowerbeds, or woods. Some women concealed valuables under their own petticoats. Those who feared theft from their neighbors or slaves waited until the middle of the night to store their belongings in secret.

The arrival of the Union Army was as bad as the civilians expected—in some cases worse. While neither rich nor poor escaped unharmed, many Union soldiers relished the destruction of the slave economy, especially the plantation. Libraries were emptied, china smashed, sideboards spilt open with axes, and cedar chests plundered. Handsome banisters were splintered, and doors were taken off their hinges. Some soldiers tried to humiliate the "Reb women" by insisting on fancy meals served to them on china in the dining room. Graffiti was scrawled on once-immaculate parlor walls. What they could not carry away the soldiers burned—particularly cotton, fences, and outbuildings. In a few hours, Sherman's soldiers and the scavengers who followed them had reduced wealthy plantation families to beggars.

This wood-engraving (left) shows Southern civilian refugees flee-ing the approach of Union troops. The exhausted, dispirited refugees were often called "fugitives" by Northerners, with the implication that they were fleeing justice. The families themselves no doubt felt they were fleeing for their lives.

On April 2, 1865, with the Union Army on the city's outskirts, the citizens of Richmond set fire to the capital and fled before the ad-vancing Northern force could overtake them, as shown in this lithograph (below). Among the refugees was Confederate presi-dent Jefferson Davis. Davis, who was captured near Irwinville, Georgia, on May 10, paid for his role as the South's leader with two years in prison.

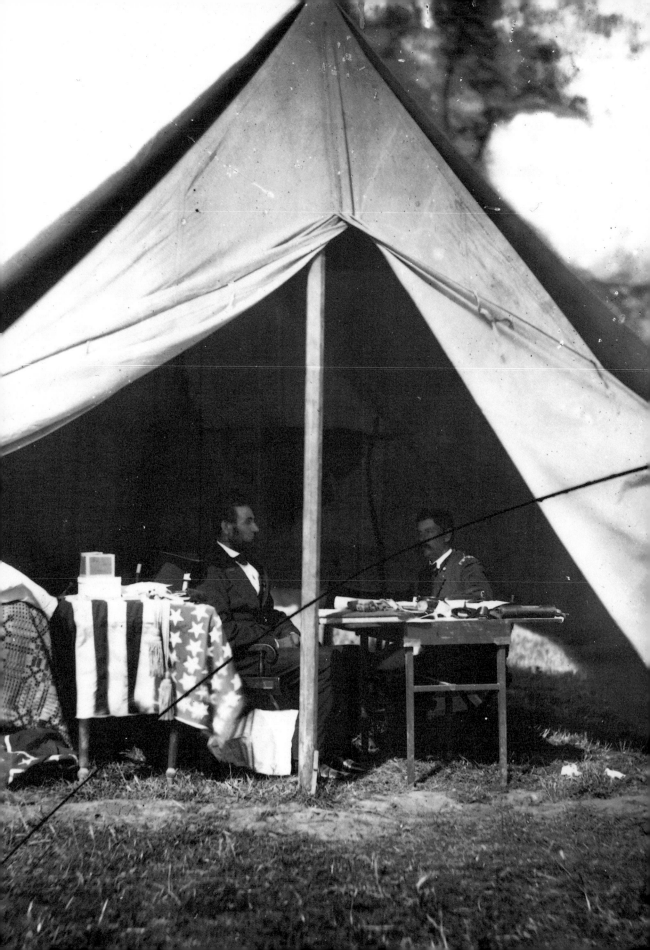

Part II
Life in the Army

On October 4, 1862, Lincoln visited General George McClellan (1826–85), commander of the Army of the Potomac, at his headquarters near Sharpsburg, Maryland. Lincoln urged McClellan to move vigorously against Robert E. Lee's Army of Northern Virginia, which McClellan's men had fought to a standstill at the Battle of Antietam. The slow, overly cautious McClellan was finally relieved of command in December.

The war was the defining event for an entire generation, in both North and South. About 2 million men served in the Union Army and Navy during the Civil War; estimates for the Confederacy range from 750,000 to 1.5 million. Oliver Wendell Holmes, Jr., a Union officer who went on to become Chief Justice of the United States, said, ". . . in our youths our hearts were touched with fire."

Ordinary soldiers on both sides of the conflict came to the battlefield believing that they were defending democracy. The typical Rebel private enlisted not to defend slavery or secession, but to oppose what he saw as the "abolitionist" invasion of his homeland. He fought for the right of self-government. As one captured Confederate infantryman put it, "I'm fighting because you're down here." The Yankee soldier fought to punish treason and preserve the Constitution, which he felt had been shamed by a lawless rebellion. And while the average soldier on each side began the war with little interest in the plight of African Americans, both described "slavery" as the condition they most feared. Each feared being enslaved to the will of the other.

"Johnny Reb" and "Billy Yank" each believed that he was the true heir to the American Revolution. The legacy of that war demanded a willingness to fight to protect liberty. But in the Civil War, American soldiers killed each other to defend vastly differing notions of what they believed liberty actually was.

RECRUITING IN THE SOUTH

Because volunteer militias had been organizing for months prior to secession, the South had an army of about 60,000 troops by the time of the crisis at Fort Sumter. On March 6, 1861, the newly established Confederate Congress authorized an army of 100,000 volunteers, who would serve for twelve months. Southern patriots responded in such numbers that the War Department had to turn away 200,000 men for lack of arms and equipment.

But Rebel enlistments fell when what was supposed to be a short, glorious war turned long and costly, and many soldiers left the army when their enlistments ended. At first, the Confederate Congress tried to promote reenlistment through rewards. In December 1861, it passed legislation granting a $50 bounty (cash bonus) and a sixty-day furlough (leave) to "one-year men" who reenlisted. But the law created more problems than it solved, with furloughs weakening the army at decisive moments in the war.

Robert E. Lee called the reward program "highly disastrous," and urged Congress to consider conscription—a draft requiring military service. On April 16, 1862, the Confederate Congress passed the first conscription act in U.S. history. Many Southerners were enraged by the bill. They believed it violated the liberty they were fighting to protect. Also, the law favored wealthy planters by exempting from the draft one white man for every twenty slaves on a plantation. This led many to call the rebellion a "rich man's war and a poor man's fight."

Both North and South used a "carrot and stick" approach to raising troops. For the most part, the tactic worked, prompting citizens to volunteer for service to avoid being "taken" as conscripts, as this Tennessee poster shows (right).

South Carolina gentlemen visit the firing range of the city's former U.S. Ordnance Depot in this wood-engraving (below), sharpening their skills for the war ahead. There were more Southerners than Northerners who had experience riding horses, handling weapons, and living outdoors, giving the Confederate armies an advantage in the field.

FREEMEN!
AVOID CONSCRIPTION!

The undersigned desires to raise a Company for the Confederate States service, and for that purpose I call upon the people of the Counties of Jefferson and Hawkins, Tenn., to meet promptly at Russellville, on SATURDAY, JULY 19th, 1862, and organize a Company.

By so doing you will avoid being taken as Conscripts, for that Act will now be enforced by order of the War Department. Rally, then, my Countrymen, to your Country's call.

S. M. DENNISON,
Of the Confederate States Army.

CHARLESTON, Tenn., JUNE 30, 1862.

When the war broke out, recruiting drives were often informal, high-spirited affairs. Here, a marching band (right) leads the way down the main street of Woodstock, Virginia, as local men join in the procession and prepare to enlist in the Confederate ranks.

Volunteer regiments in the South took pride in their distinctive names and colorful (but usually impractical) uniforms. Often, a regiment's name came from the community where it was recruited or the officer who had raised it. These included the Tallapoosa Grays, the Floyd Rifles, and the Lexington Wildcats. Pictured below are Major Roberdeau Wheat's battalion of Louisiana Zouaves, commonly called Wheat's Tigers. Wheat survived a near-fatal wound in the First Battle of Bull Run, only to die in the Peninsular Campaign a year later.

RECRUITING IN THE NORTH

In the weeks after the attack on Fort Sumter, there were more eager Northerners volunteering for the Union Army than the federal government could arm, feed, or uniform. But by 1862, the once-enthusiastic ranks were weary of battle. Voluntary enlistments fell sharply. The Union government would spend the rest of the war passing laws to tempt men into the service.

On July 17, 1862, Congress passed a law redefining the state militia. The law stated that the militia must include all able-bodied men between eighteen and thirty-five. More important, it gave the president the power to call state militia into federal service for up to nine months. The militia legislation paved the way for the Enrollment Act of 1863, a full-blown draft that required military service of all able-bodied men between the ages of twenty and forty-five. Those who could afford it were allowed to either pay the government to suspend their service, or to hire a substitute. Profits from the $300 fee were used to finance bounties for volunteers.

Conscription was unpopular, but only seven percent of the men whose names were drawn for service actually entered the Union Army. The Enrollment Act of 1863 was designed more to encourage volunteering than as a means of enforcing service. A volunteer received cash rewards amounting to more than a year's wages for the average worker, while the draftee received no benefits.

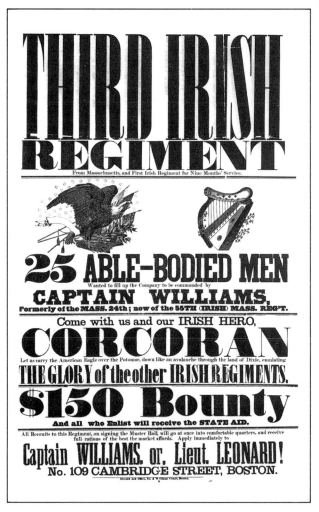

One fourth of the men who fought in the Union Army were of foreign birth or parentage. Most of these immigrant soldiers came from Germany or Ireland. This poster (above) seeks to fill vacancies in an Irish regiment being raised in Boston. Many Irish-American units had reputations for fighting both on and off the battlefield. The officers of Missouri's Irish Brigade once reported 900 fistfights breaking out in a single day—and the unit had only 800 soldiers.

The bounty system bolstered lagging enlistments by paying new recruits to volunteer. The system was plagued by "bounty jumpers," who signed up, collected their money, and then quickly deserted to sign up with a different regiment, also for cash. One man reportedly repeated the process more than thirty times before he was caught. This wood-engraving (below) shows a crowd of men in front of a recruiting office in New York City.

This wood-engraving (left) shows a no-nonsense Union volunteer of the 14th New York Regiment standing ready with bayonet fixed. As in many armies, the common soldiers of the North and South often felt more hostility toward their own officers and politicians than toward the men they were fighting. One New York private remarked that he and a friendly Rebel both wished they had "let those who made the quarrel be the ones to fight. We would restore the Union tomorrow and hang both cabinets at our earliest convenience."

In the wave of patriotism at the beginning of the war, enlistment was so popular that underage boys lied to get in. Some boys would pencil the number "18" on their boots. If the recruiting officer asked if they were "over" eighteen, they could honestly answer yes. This recruiting office in Boston (below), showing little activity, was typical of recruiting efforts after the first year of the war, when joining the army no longer seemed like a carefree adventure.

A regiment of "Yankee Doodles" marches into Dixie in this fanciful Northern lithograph. Actual Northern regiments were not so well dressed. The lithograph, like many produced in both the Union and the Confederacy, draws a connection between the Revolutionary War and the Civil War by making a reference to the Revolutionary War song "Yankee Doodle Dandy."

CAMP LIFE IN THE NORTH

Like his Confederate counterpart, the Northern recruit signed up believing that the war would be not only glorious but fun. The bad food and endless boredom of life in camp quickly soured these high expectations. As one listless recruit put it, "The first thing in the morning is drill, then drill, then drill again. Between drills, we drill. And sometimes stop to eat a little." A little food was all most men could stomach. While the Union Army's food was generally better than Confederate rations (or at least more plentiful), it was still poor. Companies were issued staples of flour, salt pork or fresh beef, beans, potatoes, and coffee, and left to cook for themselves. On the march, rations were limited to salt pork, coffee, and hardtack—hard, flavorless square crackers. Barely edible when freshly baked, aged hardtack was prone to infestation by weevils. Experienced soldiers advised that it was best eaten in the dark.

The sutler's cart provided some relief. Sutlers were civilian merchants who accompanied the army. They charged high prices for such luxuries as writing paper, cakes and pies, and raw whiskey. Drinking was an all-too-popular means of escape from the boredom and discomfort of camp and the terror of the battlefield. The results of drinking were dangerous, particularly when officers were too drunk to lead properly in battle.

A woman, perhaps the wife of an officer or an agent of the U.S. Sanitary Commission, visits Union headquarters at Miner's Hill, Virginia, in this photograph (above). From their stern faces, the surrounding soldiers don't appear to appreciate her calling. Some Union soldiers, however, approved of the presence of women in their camps: "Their influence softens and humanizes much that might otherwise be harsh and repulsive," wrote one man. "In their company, at least, officers who should be gentlemen do not get drunk."

Union soldiers break the doldrums of winter camp in this Edwin Forbes sketch. One soldier improvises on a fiddle made from a cigar box while his audience rests against a mud chimney. Their quarters consist of a tent set into a log foundation. Nearby shelters feature chimneys made of twigs, clay, and barrels.

Alexander Gardner took this photograph of members of the U.S. Christian Commission at a Union camp near German-town, Maryland, in September 1863. The organization, established by the Y.M.C.A. in 1861, helped regimental chaplains and provided small comforts for the troops, including books "of a spiritual nature."

A Siesta.

A Bucktail.

Beef Steak. Rare!

Taking it easy.
The Cavalry Skirmish Line.

Edwin Forbes

Skraggler.

An Orderly.

This series of sketches shows scenes from camp life in a Union artillery unit—including "taking a siesta" in the shade of a gun carriage. At upper right, a man fries a beefsteak over a campfire. Northern armies were usually accompanied by herds of cattle, which could be slaughtered for rations when necessary.

CAMP LIFE IN THE SOUTH

The Confederate soldier had to endure the same boredom and discomfort as the Yankee, but with less food and fewer comforts. The Rebel soldier was often forced to sleep in the open under a blanket and to march in a tattered homespun uniform. And unless he could take shoes from a dead or captured Yankee, he usually fought barefoot. Confiscated Union weapons also made up much of the South's arsenal. According to a popular story, a captured Rebel being led past a Union artillery battery remarked, "Why, you all have almost as many guns marked 'U.S.' as we do."

Gambling was a favorite distraction in both Northern and Southern camps. Baseball, a relatively new game in the 1860s, was also popular. One Southern regiment held louse races, making one of the war's most common annoyances a form of entertainment. Each soldier put a louse on a tin plate, and the first louse to crawl off was declared the winner. (One clever Confederate always won by heating his dish.)

Southern soldiers also engaged in less exotic forms of entertainment. They wrote and staged their own plays, often making fun of the Yankees. And they sang. Occasionally, unexpected concerts were held across the lines on evenings between battles. The Union regiment's band would play "Yankee Doodle" and then the Southerns would break into "Dixie." Usually the concert closed with a tune both armies could appreciate: "Home, Sweet Home."

This orderly, comfortable-looking Confederate bivouac (above) outside Corinth, Mississippi, wasn't typical of Southern camps. The fast-moving Rebel forces traveled light and rarely carried tents. Carlton McCarthy, a Confederate artilleryman, noted that the men got used to lack of shelter: "They found that life in the open air hardened them to such an extent that changes in temperature were not felt to any degree."

Confederate soldiers on picket duty cook a meal in this photograph (right). Pickets were sentries posted outside the camp to watch for enemy troops or to warn of an impending attack. Pickets were under orders to stay awake at all times, and soldiers who failed to do so were occasionally executed.

DISCIPLINE AND PUNISHMENT

Military discipline did not come easily to the volunteer soldier of the Civil War. Both Rebel and Yankee soldiers considered it degrading and "un-American" to obey orders without question. Often they had elected their commanders themselves. Many of these officers had political ambitions and thus were eager to be liked. As a result, discipline was often lax.

By early 1862, many of the more incompetent "political" officers had been weeded out by Northern examining boards. Their replacements created stiff punishments for a variety of common offenses: insolence, cowardice in battle, laziness, and theft. Insolent soldiers were tied to trees, sometimes gagged with a bandana. Cowards were shaved bald and driven out of camp in disgrace, sporting signs that read COWARD in bold letters across their bare backs. The most serious offense was desertion, which carried the death penalty. Widespread in both armies, desertion was far more frequent among drafted troops than volunteers. In the North, Lincoln responded by issuing a general amnesty on March 10, 1863, promising deserters that they would not be punished if they returned to their units by April 1, 1863.

Union firing squads executed 141 soldiers for desertion; figures for the Confederate Army are not known. Both Abraham Lincoln and Jefferson Davis, however, suspended the death sentences of many deserters.

Drunken brawls and fights over gambling plagued both armies. General George McClellan once remarked that "total abstinence" from drinking would be worth 50,000 men to the Union cause. In this photograph (above), Confederate troops take a leisurely break for poker, liquor, and pipe.

This drawing (opposite, top) pokes fun at the punishment given to two soldiers with a fondness for gambling. Although forced to wear signs on their backs, the two petty criminals are already back at the gaming table—while an unconcerned sentry looks on.

This lithograph (right) shows a typical Union military execution involving a Pennsylvania private convicted of desertion and "highway robbery." With his regiment watching, the condemned man was marched to the place of execution, blindfolded, and then seated on a coffin. The execution was carried out by a firing squad of twelve men, chosen by drawing lots. The body was usually buried in an unmarked grave.

General Potrick's punishment for Gamblers — A R Waud

AFRICAN AMERICANS IN THE MILITARY

African Americans lobbied hard to be allowed to serve in the Union Army. Frederick Douglass, for example, argued that blacks had served in both the Revolutionary War and the War of 1812. Politicians and the press, however, claimed that this was a "white man's war." But by late 1862, enlistments were at an all-time low. Northern prejudice finally gave way to practicality, and the enlistment of black troops in the Union Army began.

Black soldiers served under especially harsh conditions. The Confederacy had threatened to enslave or execute captured black soldiers and their officers. On April 12, 1864, the worst fears of many were confirmed. Confederate general Nathan Bedford Forrest captured Fort Pillow, a Union garrison in Tennessee. The fort was manned by about 570 troops, of whom just less than half were black. Forrest's men massacred dozens of unarmed black soldiers and some whites. Said Forrest, "It is hoped that these facts will demonstrate . . . that Negro soldiers cannot cope with Southerners."

In the South, opposition to the enlistment of slaves was universal. Desperate for reinforcements, Robert E. Lee wrote to Jefferson Davis on March 15, 1865, requesting slave troops who would be freed at the end of the war. The Confederate Congress authorized the enlistment, leaving their future as slaves up to the states, but few black soldiers saw service before Lee's surrender at Appomattox.

The Confederacy used slaves as laborers throughout the war, but refused to enlist them as soldiers until a few weeks before the war's end. "The day you make soldiers of them is the beginning of the end of the revolution," said Georgia politician Howell Cobb. "If slaves will make good soldiers, then our whole theory of slavery is wrong." Slaves work to mount a cannon in preparation for the attack on Fort Sumter in this watercolor (right).

The North's black soldiers faced prejudice within their own ranks as well as from Confederates. Until 1864, black soldiers were paid less than whites. White officers commanded black units, but many whites refused such duty. According to one general, there was "a stupid, unreasoning, and quite vengeful prejudice . . . among the regular officers" against black troops. Shown here (below) is Company E of the 4th U.S. Colored Infantry. The unit fought heroically in the opening days of the Petersburg Campaign in June 1864.

THE PRESS IN THE FIELD

Americans were hungry for information about the war's progress. A new breed of journalist—the "special" or military artist—was created to meet this demand. These pictorial journalists were graphic artists who were sent to the front to sketch eyewitness accounts of the war. Their sketches were then rushed back to editorial offices, where woodblock engravings were made from the originals. During the four-year conflict, over thirty special artists covered all aspects of the soldier's life, from the sutler's cart to combat. Some of these journalists were acclaimed for their realism and artistry, bringing a larger audience to the journals for which they reported. Winslow Homer and Arthur R. Waud, both special artists for *Harper's Weekly*, were the most famous.

The Southern press was smaller than its Union counterpart. Some of the Confederate newspapers that managed to stay afloat in the wake of severe shortages functioned as government mouthpieces. One Richmond paper claimed to rely on smuggled Northern newspapers for its battle coverage, because the Confederate government wanted to downplay the South's growing casualties.

European newspaper correspondents also reported from American battlefields. Perhaps the best known was William Russell of the pro-Southern *London Times*, whose nickname was "Bull Run Russell" after publishing an article criticizing the Union Army's performance in the First Battle of Bull Run.

The Southern Illustrated News *announces Lee's appointment as commander in chief of all Confederate forces (above). Lee is pictured here as a vital young man. In fact, Lee was fifty-six years old and gray-bearded at the time. Accuracy wasn't overly important to some publishers, in North and South. Lithographers sometimes used a single scene to depict different battles, changing uniform colors and other details as necessary.*

In this photograph, reporters from the New York Herald set up shop on the march with the Union Army. Reporters weren't welcome in all Union headquarters. William Tecumseh Sherman hated journalists, after reports that he was insane circulated in 1862. Later in the war, Ulysses S. Grant told reporters traveling with the Army of the Potomac that he would help them obtain "all proper information," but, according to journalist Junius Browne, the Union commander was "not very communicative."

The elegant detail of Winslow Homer's work is shown in this portrait of a Union sharpshooter on picket duty. The soldier rests his rifle on a branch, steadying himself with his hand, his canteen hooked on a twig. Homer is so exacting that he clearly catches the white of the sharpshooter's eye, fierce with concentration.

Winslow Homer (1836–1910) made this sketch of his colleague, English-born Arthur Waud, at work. Using an empty barrel as a chair and his knee as an easel, Waud stares intently at his subjects—soldiers in a Maine regiment—while sketching. Waud's brother William also produced some notable depictions of battles and army life.

PHOTOGRAPHY IN THE WAR

The Civil War marked one of the first times the reality of war was recorded by the camera. (Actual battlefield shots were rare, however, because of the long exposure time required by early cameras.) The photographer lurched onto the field in a large wagon that served as a portable darkroom. Next he readied the "big black box," a camera the size of a milk crate and several times as heavy. The picture taken, he raced back to the wagon to start developing the large glass plates before the image faded beyond recognition.

The most famous of all Civil War photographers was Mathew B. Brady, a New Yorker who covered the conflict from Bull Run to Richmond at his own expense. Brady's ever-present wagon and crew were known by curious troops as the "What-is-It" wagon. Brady produced over 3,500 photos of the war, although many of them were taken by his talented assistants and colleagues, including Timothy H. O'Sullivan and Alexander Gardner.

Brady's efforts left him bankrupt, and after the war his negatives were sold to pay his debts. Eventually, the Library of Congress obtained most of the surviving photographs. The Brady photographs are the richest source of visual information about the Civil War that exists today.

Photographer Samuel Cooley and his crew stand beside their photographic wagon (right), along with a typical camera on its sturdy tripod. Many of the fragile glass plates of lesser-known photographers like Cooley were lost or destroyed after the war. Occasionally, however, forgotten Civil War photographs come to light. In 1964, for example, the Library of Congress obtained a long-lost series of views of the siege of Charleston, South Carolina, by the photographers Haas & Peale.

Mathew Brady (c. 1823–96; in top hat, below) poses next to General Samuel P. Heintzelman on the steps of the former Lee mansion in Arlington, Virginia. Brady exhibited photographs of the carnage of the Battle of Antietam in New York City in October 1862. The grim, haunting photographs (actually taken by Alexander Gardner) stunned viewers. One wrote: "Mr. Brady has brought home the terrible earnestness of war. If he has not brought bodies and laid them in our dooryards, he has done something very like it."

MEDICINE

Disease was a greater threat to soldiers than combat. For every Union or Confederate soldier killed on the battlefield, two more were felled by diseases such as cholera, typhoid, and dysentery. Yet if a soldier was wounded and survived, he might face a lifetime of suffering. The heavy-caliber, soft-lead bullets of Civil War rifles inflicted terrible wounds. A hit to the leg or arm usually shattered the bone and carried away so much flesh that amputation was necessary. Surgeons' tents with piles of amputated limbs outside were a common sight after every battle.

The Civil War occurred before the discovery of many of the basics of modern medicine. Doctors in the 1860s were unaware that dangerous organisms could infect water and food and could enter the bloodstream through open wounds. They had no knowledge of the relationship between sterilized instruments and infection. Many surgeons reportedly sharpened their scalpels on their bootsoles just before operating.

In spite of these limitations, many new medical practices were introduced during the war. In the Union Army, a special ambulance corps was trained for on-the-spot first aid and speedy evacuation of the wounded to field hospitals.

While the Confederacy was hampered by a shortage of supplies, the efforts of Southern women and civilian doctors saved countless lives. The largest hospital on either side, in fact, was Richmond's Chimborazo Hospital, which could house over 10,000.

This print (opposite, top) shows several scenes in the Citizen's Volunteer Hospital in Philadelphia. One of the largest Union medical establishments, the Citizen's Hospital was established and staffed solely through the labors of civilians. Northern civilians also operated hospital ships in Southern ports and rivers, usually staffed with doctors and nurses from the U.S. Sanitary Commission.

In this photograph (right), Union surgeons stand outside the Seminary Hospital in Washington, while two nurses look on through a window. Although doctors in both the Union and Confederate armies did the best they could for the wounded and sick, the poor state of medical science led many soldiers to fear them. In 1862, an Alabama soldier wrote, "I believe the doctors kill more than they cure . . . Doctors ain't got half-sense."

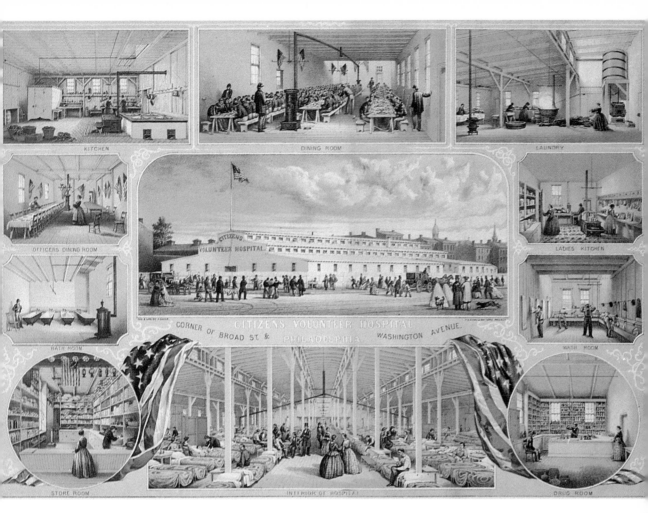

KITCHEN

DINING ROOM

LAUNDRY

OFFICERS DINING ROOM

CITIZENS VOLUNTEER HOSPITAL

LADIES KITCHEN

BATH ROOM

CITIZENS VOLUNTEER HOSPITAL
CORNER OF BROAD ST. & WASHINGTON AVENUE. PHILADELPHIA

WASH ROOM

STORE ROOM

INTERIOR OF HOSPITAL

DRUG ROOM

Clara Barton (1821–1912; left) was a patent office clerk when the war began. Acting independently of government authorities, she single-handedly raised funds for vital medicines, then supervised their use at the front. She also oversaw the creation of a cemetery for Union soldiers who had died at the Andersonville prison camp in Georgia. After the war, she founded the American Red Cross and served as its first president.

As this fanciful lithograph (below) shows, the women who tended the wounded in the thick of battle were considered angels by the troops. At first, women were refused access to battlefields. Northern nurse Mother Bickerdyke, however, would not retreat. When asked on what authority she acted, she replied "I am here on the authority of God."

Volunteers assisting the wounded on the field of Battle

In major battles, casualties often overwhelmed the small medical detachments. This drawing by A. R. Waud shows Maryland civilians helping to transport wounded soldiers from a Union field hospital after the Battle of Antietam in September 1862. Surgeons working close to the front lines often became casualties themselves. "Some medical officers lost their lives in their devotion to duty in the battle of Antietam," reported General Jonathan Letterman, the Army of the Potomac's medical director.

PRISONERS

In 1862, the Confederate and Union armies agreed to exchange prisoners periodically. But once the Confederate Congress authorized the enslavement of captured black soldiers in May 1863, the Union War Department stopped the exchange.

This change in policy soon caused extreme overcrowding in prisons on both sides. By 1864, prison camps were rightly seen as death traps worse than the bloodiest battlefield. Andersonville, a Confederate prison outside Macon, Georgia, earned an unmatched reputation for suffering. Opened in February 1864, Andersonville was built on sixteen acres and designed to hold 10,000 total prisoners. By August, the prison's population had swelled to 33,000. Although an additional ten acres were added, this still left only thirty-four square feet per man. When an Atlanta newspaper reported that 300 Yankees died at Andersonville in a single hot day—adding "we thank heaven for such blessings"—the Northern public was outraged. Angry Northerners wrote editorials calling for retaliation, urging reciprocal treatment of Southern prisoners held in Union camps. President Lincoln, however, refused to match cruelty with cruelty.

Andersonville was an extreme example of problems common to prisons in both the North and South. Confederate soldiers perished at an alarming rate in Northern prisons such as Johnson's Island and Elmira. For both sides, the treatment of captive soldiers became one of the most emotional issues of the war.

These gaunt Confederates (above) were photographed just after their capture in the Battle of Gettysburg in July 1863. In the early years of the war, prisoners were exchanged regularly. Others were paroled—allowed to return home after swearing an oath not to rejoin the army—until formally exchanged for a soldier held by the opposing forces.

Rations for prisoners at Andersonville were limited to a half cup of corn meal and two teaspoons of sugar per day. The wood-engravings shown here (opposite, top) of an Andersonville survivor were based on actual photographs taken at United States General Hospital at Annapolis, Maryland. They were used as evidence in the postwar trial of Captain Henry Wirz, the camp's commander, who was accused of mistreating Union prisoners. The Swiss-born Wirz was hanged —the only officer on either side to be executed for war crimes.

This view (right) clearly shows the terrible overcrowding at Andersonville. The conditions at this and other prisons in both the Union and the Confederacy weren't caused by a deliberate policy of cruelty. The number of prisoners on both sides, especially after the practice of exchanges and paroles ended, simply overwhelmed both governments. The result was overcrowding, suffering, and death.

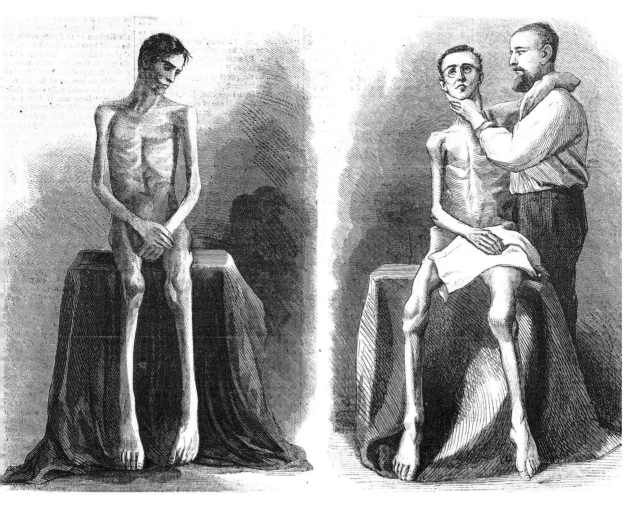

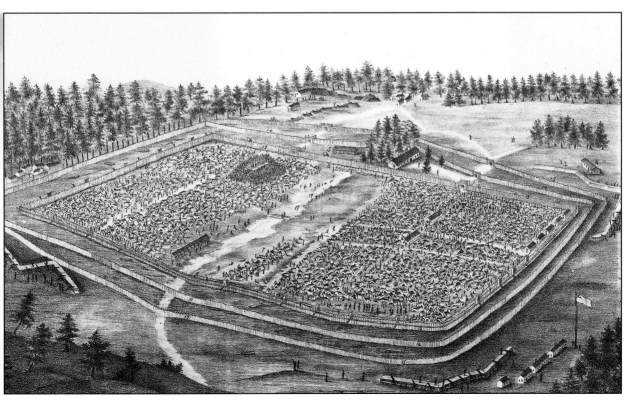

Resource Guide

Key to picture positions: (T) top, (C) center, (B) bottom; and in combinations: (TL) top left, (TR) top right, (BL) bottom left, (BR) bottom right, (RC) right center, (LC) left center.

Key to picture locations within the Library of Congress collections (and where available, photo negative numbers): P - Prints and Photographs Division; R - Rare Book Division; G - General Collections; MSS - Manuscript Division; G&M - Geography Division

PICTURES IN THIS VOLUME

2–3 flag, P 4–5 label, P 6–7 family, P 8–9 map, G

Timeline: 10–11 TL, Victoria, G; TR, hospital, P, B8184-10369; BR, Baker, P 12–13 BL, fort, G; TR, Douglass, P, BH832-30219 14–15 BL, ironclads, P; TR, Vallandigham, G 16–17 TL, troops, P, B8171-7890; BR, Charleston, P, USZ62-42046

Part I: 18–19 farm, P 20–21 TL, Ruffin, G; BR, boat, G 22–23 TL, Davis, G; TR, convention, G; BR, cabinet, P, USZ62-5263 24–25 C, Capitol, P, BH-823401; BR, cabinet, P, USA7-25808 26–27 TR, Frietchie, P, USZ61-329; BR, Baltimore, P 28–29 BL, house, P, USZ62-92583; TR, Ellsworth, P 30–31 TR, bond, MSS; C, factory, P, B8171-7542 32–33 TL, map, G; BL, boats, G; BR, cartoon, P, USZ61-146 34–35 TR, factory, G; C, harbor, P 36–37 BL, wagon, P, B8171-518; TR, slaves, P, B8171-383; BR, hiding, G 38–39 TL, Douglass, P, USZ62-15887; TR, man reading, P 40–41 C, Lincoln, P, USZC4-1425 42–43 BL, train, P, USZ62-12791; TR, Vallandigham, P, USZ62-42029; BR, draft riots, P, USZ62-41234 44–45 TL, broadside, MSS; TR, cartridge factory, P, USZ62-32165; BR, field hospital, P, B8184-4092 46–47 TL, sewing, P, USZ62-15693; TR, riot, P, USZ62-47636; BR, burial, R 48–49 TL, broadside, MSS; TR, Farragut, P, USZ62-85797; BR, river, P 50–51 TL, Battle Hymn, MSS; TR, Hail! Glorious, P; BR, Our National, P, USZ62-33407 52–53 TL,

knight, P; TR, tobacco label, P; BR, ointment, P, USZ62-724 54–55 TL, Boyd, P, BH82401-4864; TR, hotel, P, USZC2-1289; BR, Webster, G 56–57 TL, Lincoln, P, USZ62-7542; TR, inauguration, P, USZ62-279; BR, voting, P, USZ62-1063 58–59 TL, Vicksburg, P; TR, looting, G; BR, woods, G 60–61 TL, fleeing, G; C, Richmond, P

Part II: 62–63 tent, P, B8171-7948 64–65 TR, broadside, P, USZ62-39368; C, target practice, G 66–67 TR, band, P, USZ62-16608; C, Zouaves, P, B818-10045 68–69 TL, poster, P, USZ62-40807; BR, office, P 70–71 TL, soldier, G; BL, office, P, USZ62-31233; BR, marching band, P 72–73 C, headquarters, P, B8184-4108; BR, violin, P, USZ62-14188 74–75 BL, Christian Commission, P, B8171-7471; TR, camp scenes, P, USZ62-13948 76–77 C, camp, P; BR, picket duty, P, B8184-4390 78–79 TL, gambling, P, USZ62-7145; TR, punishment, P, USZ62-14781; BR, execution, P, USZ62-15670 80–81 TR, cannon, P, USZC4-690; C, soldiers, P, B8171-7890 82–83 TL, Lee, G; BR, newspaper wagon, P, B8171-7235 84–85 TL, sharpshooter, G; BR, Waud, P, USZ62-39448 86–87 TR, wagon, P, B8171-4018; C, Brady, P, B811-2304 88–89 TR, hospital scenes, P; BR, surgeons, P, B8171-7875 90–91 TL, Barton, P, USZ62-19319; BL, nurse, P; TR, stretchers, P 92–93 TL, prisoners, P; TR, starved man, P, USZ62-703; BR, prison, P, USZ62-17090

SUGGESTED READING

BOWEN, JOHN. *Civil War Days*. Secaucus, N.J.: Chartwell Books, Inc., 1987.
CATTON, BRUCE. *The American Heritage Picture History of the Civil War*. New York: Bonanza Books, 1982.

CHANNING, STEVEN A. *Confederate Ordeal: The Southern Home Front*. Alexandria, Virginia: Time-Life Books, 1984.
SMITH, CARTER. *The Civil War*. New York: Facts on File, 1989.
TIME-LIFE. *Brother Against Brother*. New York: Prentice Hall, 1990.

Index

Page numbers in *italics* indicate illustrations